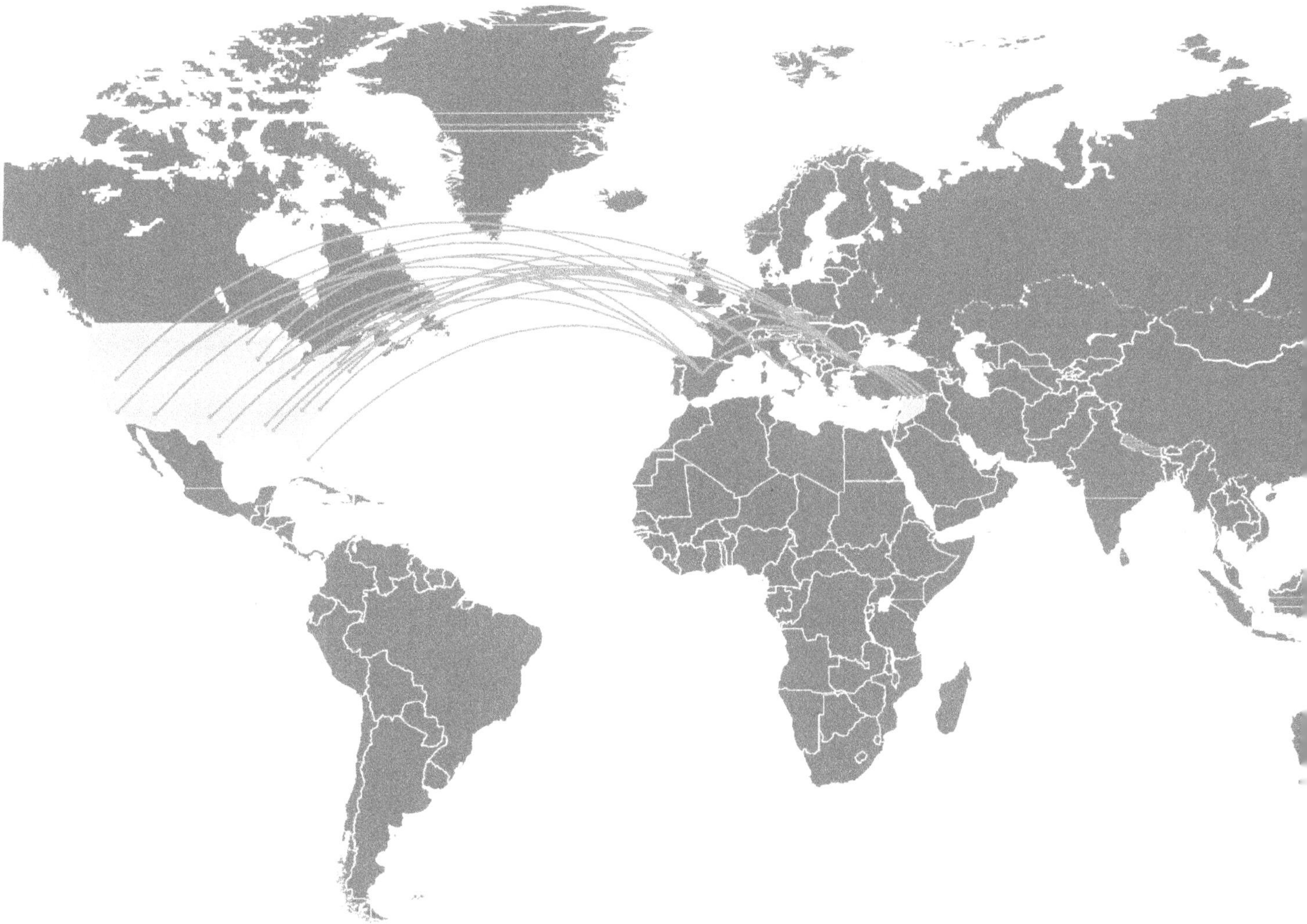

In March 2015, the U.S. House of Representatives Homeland Security Committee launched a bipartisan Task Force on Combating Terrorist and Foreign Fighter Travel. Eight Members of Congress were charged with examining the threat to the United States from "foreign fighters"—individuals who leave home, travel abroad to terrorist safe havens, and join or assist violent extremist groups. The Task Force assessed domestic and overseas efforts to obstruct terrorist travel, as well as security gaps. This is their final report.

The Task Force would like to thank the many individuals and organizations who made the review possible. While some are not listed by name in this report, their inputs were not forgotten and helped shape the findings and recommendations contained herein. Most importantly, the Task Force would like to thank the many staff members who contributed to the final product for their hard work and dedication to country.

CONTENT

Introduction

- The Global Surge in Foreign Fighters
- The Danger of Foreign Fighters: Recruits, "Returnees," and Remote Radicalization
- Americans on the Pathway to Terror

Key Findings & Recommendations

- Watchlisting
- Information Sharing
- Prevention Activities

- Pre-Travel Phase
- Travel Phase

Appendices

HOMELAND SECURITY COMMITTEE TASK FORCE
on
COMBATING TERRORIST AND FOREIGN FIGHTER TRAVEL

Chairman Michael McCaul
Texas

Ranking Member Bennie Thompson
Mississippi

Republican Lead John Katko
New York

Democratic Lead Loretta Sanchez
California

Rep. Barry Loudermilk
Georgia

Rep. Filemon Vela
Texas

Rep. John Ratcliffe
Texas

Rep. Donald Payne
New Jersey

Rep. Will Hurd
Texas

Rep. Martha McSally
Arizona

Miles Taylor, Republican Staff Lead
Nicole Tisdale, Democratic Staff Lead

Special thanks to Committee Staff who contributed to this final report:

Paul Anstine, Lanier Avant, Kate Bonvechio, Mandy Bowers, Adam Comis, Cate Cullen, Moira Bergin, Luke Burke, Alan Carroll, Paige Davies, Steven Giaier, Katy Flynn, Laura Fullerton, Hope Goins, Cedric Haynes, Kerry Kinirons, Kyle Klein, Vanessa Layne, Tyler Lowe, Kyle McFarland, Jason Miller, John Neal, Ramzi Nemo, Leaksmy Norin, Alison Northrop, Joan O'Hara, Jason Olin, Christopher Schepis, Brendan Shields, Andrea Thompson, Claire Woolf, and Maseh Zarif.

For if there was ever a challenge in our interconnected world that cannot be met by any one nation alone, it is this: terrorists crossing borders and threatening to unleash unspeakable violence. These terrorists believe our countries will be unable to stop them. The safety of our citizens demand that we do.

PRESIDENT BARACK OBAMA

SEPTEMBER 2014

Foreign fighters traveling to Syria or Iraq could, for example, gain battlefield experience and increased exposure to violent extremist elements ... they may use these skills and exposure to radical ideology to return to their countries of origin, including the United States, to conduct attacks on the Homeland.

SEPTEMBER 2014

This is a global crisis in need of a global solution. The Syrian conflict has turned that region into a cradle of violent extremism. But the world cannot simply sit back and let it become a training ground from which our nationals can return and launch attacks.

JULY 2014

EXECUTIVE SUMMARY

Threat Environment

Today we are witnessing the largest global convergence of jihadists in history, as individuals from more than 100 countries have migrated to the conflict zone in Syria and Iraq since 2011.[1] Some initially flew to the region to join opposition groups seeking to oust Syrian dictator Bashar al-Assad, but most are now joining the Islamic State of Iraq and Syria (ISIS), inspired to become a part of the group's "caliphate" and to expand its repressive society. Over 25,000 foreign fighters have traveled to the battlefield to enlist with Islamist terrorist groups, including at least 4,500 Westerners. More than 250 individuals from the United States have also joined or attempted to fight with extremists in the conflict zone.[2]

These fighters pose a serious threat to the United States and its allies. Armed with combat experience and extremist connections, many of them are only a plane-flight away from our shores. Even if they do not return home to plot attacks, foreign fighters have taken the lead in recruiting a new generation of terrorists and are seeking to radicalize Westerners online to spread terror back home.

Task Force on Combating Terrorist and Foreign Fighter Travel

Responding to the growing threat, the House Homeland Security Committee established the Task Force on Combating Terrorist and Foreign Fighter Travel in March 2015. Chairman Michael McCaul and Ranking Member Bennie Thompson appointed a bipartisan group of eight lawmakers charged with reviewing the threat to the United States from foreign fighters, examining the government's preparedness to respond to a surge in terrorist travel, and providing a final report with findings and recommendations to address the challenge. Members and staff also assessed security measures in other countries, as U.S. defenses depend partly on whether foreign governments are able to interdict extremists before they reach our shores.

Results of the Review

The Task Force makes *32 key findings* and provides accompanying recommendations, which can be read in full starting in the second part of this report. Among other conclusions reached, the Task Force finds that:

- Despite concerted efforts to stem the flow, we have largely failed to stop Americans from traveling overseas to join jihadists. Of the hundreds of Americans who have sought to travel to the conflict zone in Syria and Iraq, authorities have only interdicted a fraction of them. Several dozen have also managed to make it back into America.
- The U.S. government lacks a national strategy for combating terrorist travel and has not produced one in nearly a decade.
- The unprecedented speed at which Americans are being radicalized by violent extremists is straining federal law enforcement's ability to monitor and intercept suspects.
- Jihadist recruiters are increasingly using secure websites and apps to communicate with Americans, making it harder for law enforcement to disrupt plots and terrorist travel.
- There is currently no comprehensive global database of foreign fighter names. Instead, countries including the United States rely on a patchwork system for swapping extremist identities, increasing the odds foreign fighters will slip through the cracks.
- "Broken travel" and other evasive transit tactics are making it harder to track foreign fighters.
- Few initiatives exist nationwide to raise awareness about foreign-fighter recruitment and to assist communities with spotting warning signs.
- The federal government has failed to develop clear early-intervention strategies—or "off-ramps" to radicalization—to prevent suspects already on law enforcement's radar from leaving to fight with extremists.
- Gaping security weaknesses overseas—especially in Europe—are putting the U.S. homeland in danger by making it easier for aspiring foreign fighters to migrate to terrorist hotspots and for jihadists to return to the West.
- Despite improvements since 9/11, foreign partners are still sharing information about terrorist suspects in a manner which is ad hoc, intermittent, and often incomplete.
- Ultimately, severing today's foreign-fighter flows depends on eliminating the problem at the source in Syria and Iraq and, in the long run, preventing the emergence of additional terrorist sanctuaries.

The Task Force's final report is divided into two primary sections. The *Introduction* provides background on the foreign fighter phenomenon, an assessment of why it is a threat to the United States, and an analysis of 58 case studies of Americans who traveled or attempted to travel to fight in Syria and Iraq. The *Key Findings & Recommendations* section outlines the Task Force's main conclusions and is sub-divided into four parts: (1) U.S. government strategy and planning to combat the threat; (2) efforts to identify terrorist and foreign fighters -- and prevent them from traveling; (3) efforts to detect and disrupt terrorists and foreign fighters when they travel; and (4) overseas security gaps.

NOTES ON METHODOLOGY

The Task Force conducted the investigation over a six month period. Its final report is based on briefings, meetings, domestic and foreign site visits, and analysis of classified and unclassified documents. A summary of the group's activity can be found in Appendix I. The Task Force spoke with current and former federal officials throughout the national security community and at all relevant departments and agencies. The group also consulted with state and local law enforcement, outside experts, and foreign officials on several continents.

Members and staff did not examine all U.S. government efforts to stop extremists from crossing borders but instead focused on those with the most relevance to the foreign fighter threat. Nevertheless, the Task Force's review is one of the most extensive public examinations of U.S. government efforts to counter terrorist travel in the post-9/11 world. The 9/11 Commission gave considerable attention to the subject, but since then government activity in this space has expanded rapidly. The proliferation of these programs, projects, and activities is one reason the Task Force urges more regular, government-wide audits of America's defenses against terrorist travel.[3]

Where practicable, we have tried to cite publicly available sources, due to the fact that many of the Task Force's briefings were either closed to the public or classified. Our written analysis of U.S. foreign fighter case studies, for instance, relies entirely on open sources. However, some material is cited anonymously in cases where individuals were assured confidentiality in order to discuss issues more freely.

The Task Force's final report was submitted to the Chairman and the Ranking Member of the House Homeland Security Committee in September 2015 to be considered and prepared for final release.[4] Prior to publication, it was shared with the White House and all departments and agencies that cooperated with the review, partly to prevent the unauthorized disclosure of sensitive information. The Committee made technical, conforming, and other edits to the report based on agency comments and corrections.

THE THREAT

The United States and the international community face a grave and growing threat from jihadist foreign fighters. These are individuals who leave home, travel abroad to terrorist safe havens, and join or assist violent extremist groups. Today's foreign fighters are being lured overseas largely by groups like the Islamic State of Iraq and Syria (ISIS) and al Qaeda's affiliates to promote a perverse brand of militant Islamism. Not only are they strengthening terrorist armies that oppress millions, but some are also plotting attacks against the West and radicalizing new generations.

Foreign fighters have contributed to an alarming rise in global terrorism by expanding extremist networks, inciting individuals back home to conduct attacks, or by returning to carry out acts of terror themselves. For instance, one prominent British foreign fighter killed this year in Syria was linked to terrorist plots spanning the globe, from the United Kingdom to Australia, without ever having left the Middle East. [5] In another case, an American from Ohio was arrested in April after returning from Syria to plan an attack on a U.S. military base, where he intended to behead soldiers. [6] This case is part of a broader challenge. Indeed, since early 2014 more than a dozen terrorist plots against Western targets have involved so-called "returnees" from terrorist safe havens like Syria and Libya.[7]

Foreign fighters are also the motive power behind the growth of ISIS. Despite a year of U.S. and allied airstrikes, the group has held most of its territory and continues to replenish its ranks with outside recruits.[8] Military officials estimate airstrikes have killed around 10,000 extremists, but new foreign fighters replace them almost as quickly as they are killed. [9] ISIS has also grown from a single terrorist sanctuary to having a direct presence, affiliates, or groups pledging support in 18 countries. [10] The organization is believed to have inspired or directed nearly 60 terrorist plots or attacks against Western countries, including 15 in the United States. [11] Some of these were masterminded by foreign fighters based in Syria, while others were carried out by returnees themselves or homegrown extremists.

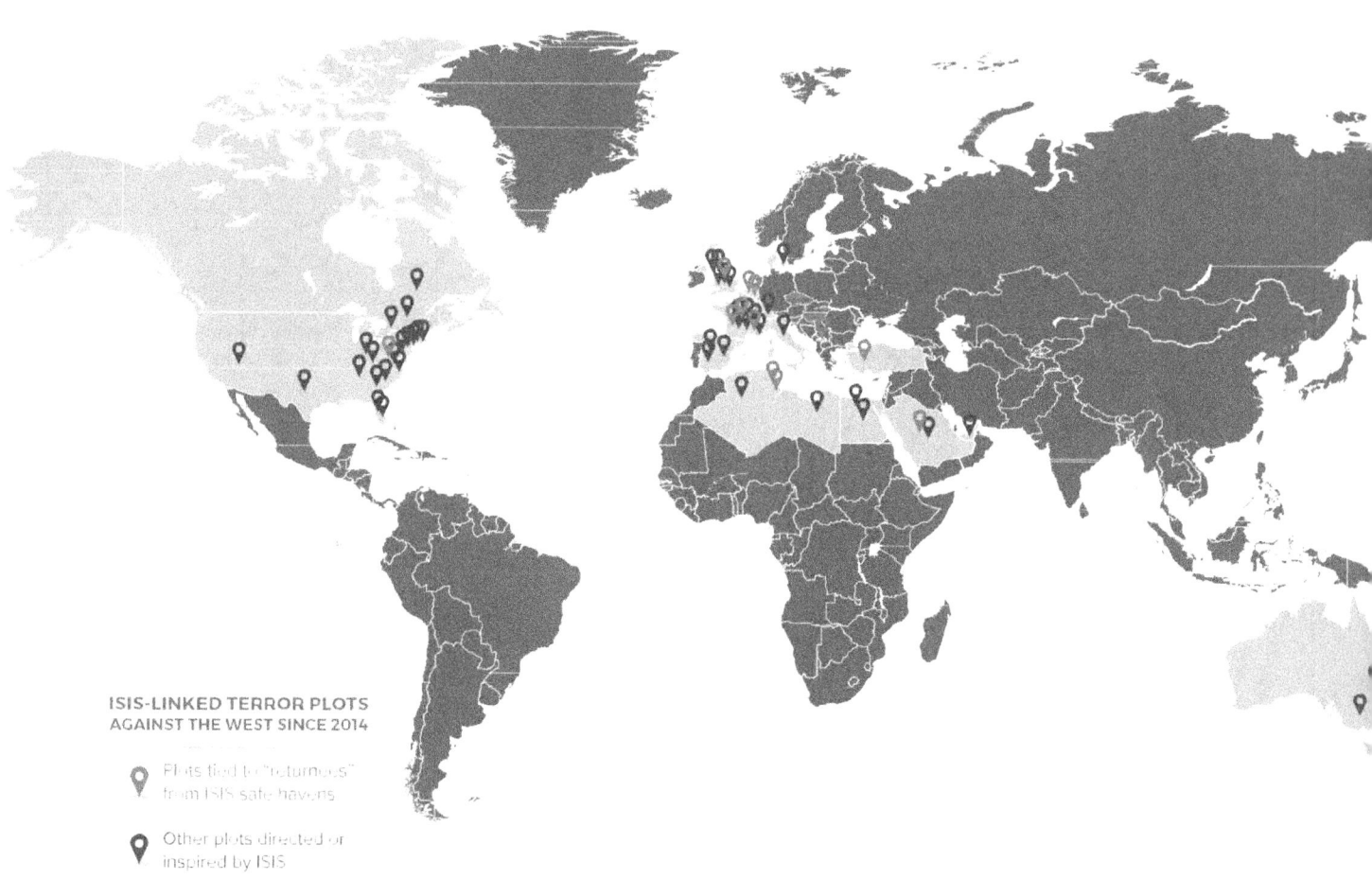

ISIS-LINKED TERROR PLOTS AGAINST THE WEST SINCE 2014

📍 Plots tied to "returnees" from ISIS safe havens

📍 Other plots directed or inspired by ISIS

The foreign fighter phenomenon is not new. For decades, Western citizens have gone to extremist hotspots to fight or train with Islamist terror groups, from Afghanistan to Somalia, and many of them have returned with nefarious intentions. Since 9/11, dozens of Americans extremists have been arrested after coming back home from terrorist safe havens, including individuals plotting attacks.[12] In 2002, for instance, American citizen Jose Padilla was arrested in Chicago for allegedly planning a "dirty bomb" attack; he had attended an al Qaeda training camp in Afghanistan in 2000. In another case, Afghan-American Najibullah Zazi traveled from New York to Pakistan and was arrested in 2009 after returning home to conduct a suicide attack on the New York City subway system. The same year Faisal Shazad went abroad and received training from the Pakistani-Taliban; he came back to the United States and was arrested after attempting a car bombing in Times Square.

FBI Director James Comey warned last year that we need to brace ourselves for a wider "terrorist diaspora" out of Syria and Iraq.

The level of terrorist travel we are seeing today, however, is without precedent. The numbers are now so high that Western governments are becoming increasingly worried they will be unable to prevent violent extremists from entering their countries undetected. Federal Bureau of Investigation (FBI) Director James Comey warned last year that we need to brace ourselves for a wider "terrorist diaspora" out of Syria and Iraq.[13] Whether directed to conduct attacks or not, many of these individuals will return with the combat experience, extremist connections, and motivations to do so. Indeed, the ripple effect of terror created by foreign fighter travel to and from Syria and Iraq, in particular, will pose a threat to America for decades to come unless dealt with quickly and decisively.

Today's explosive growth in foreign fighter travel to Syria and Iraq has surpassed other jihadist conflicts in both scope and magnitude. Travelers hail from all corners of the globe, represent an array of ethnicities, and span virtually all age ranges. While some individuals initially traveled to the region for humanitarian purposes, the overwhelming majority are now headed there because of jihadist ideology or to live in the so-called Islamic State. Migration to the conflict zone does not appear to have abated, and the threat continues to evolve as new safe havens attract additional foreign fighters.

From Afar: Foreign Recruits and the Syrian Civil War

The foreign fighter phenomenon in Syria and Iraq has its origins in the Syrian civil war. Local protests broke out in Syria in March 2011 after a group of teenagers were arrested and tortured by Syrian authorities for painting revolutionary slogans on school property.[14] Security forces opened fire on the protestors, sparking nationwide demonstrations that shifted from pro-democracy demands to calls for the Bashar al-Assad regime's ouster. By July 2011, hundreds of thousands had taken to the streets as the government tried unsuccessfully to crush the rebellion. The opposition soon took up arms to expel Assad's security forces from their local territories.[15]

The country descended into full-scale civil war by 2012. Rebel brigades assembled to fight government forces for control of cities and towns across Syria. Several high-level defectors from the regular Syrian Army formed the Free Syrian Army, attracting thousands of recruits. But the conflict devolved further as various nationalist, sectarian, and religious factions, primarily Sunnis, emerged to fight Assad's Shia Alawite government. War volunteers trickled into the country from abroad, with some traveling to support the anti-Assad insurgency and others arriving with more radical goals. Jihadist groups capitalized on the chaos and gained influence.

By 2013, the influx of foreign fighters was growing quickly. Rebel fighters on the ground appealed to the world by documenting the regime's atrocities on social media, and prominent Sunni clerics called for Muslims to travel to the war-torn country to oust Assad.[16] By summer, nearly 5,000 foreign fighters from 60 countries had arrived.[17] One scholar observed that the numbers "exceeded that of any previous conflict in the modern history of the Muslim world."[18] Although an estimated 10,000 total fighters came to Afghanistan to attack the Soviets in the 1980s, there were likely never more than 3,000 to 4,000 at any given period. [19]

By the end of 2013, analysts estimated more than 8,500 foreign fighters had flocked to Syria to fight with the anti-Assad opposition or join Sunni jihadist groups.[20] Around 70 percent were from the Middle East and North Africa, but 2,000 or so were assessed to be from Western countries.[21] U.S. intelligence and security officials grew especially alarmed about the number of extremists entering the conflict zone, which was then thought to include "dozens" of Americans.[22]

The Rise of ISIS

One jihadist group in particular saw an opening. The Islamic State of Iraq (ISI), a successor organization to al Qaeda in Iraq (AQI), called for sectarian war and the creation of a regional Islamic state.[23] AQI was a terrorist group whose leadership had pledged allegiance to Osama bin Laden in 2004 and which led an insurgency against U.S. forces in the country. After the group's leader Abu Musab al-Zarqawi was killed in a 2006 U.S. airstrike, it rebranded as ISI. The terror outfit was weakened by the surge of U.S. troops into Iraq, the Anbar awakening, and later the death of its two top leaders in 2010. With the eventual withdrawal of American forces, however, ISI took advantage of the security vacuum and Sunni disenfranchisement with the central government to ramp up attacks. Its new leader, Abu Bakr al-Baghdadi, oversaw the escalation in violence.

In April 2013, al-Baghdadi declared the creation of the Islamic State of Iraq and the Levant (hereafter, ISIS). He sought to merge his forces with those of al Qaeda's Syrian affiliate, but al Qaeda leader Ayman al-Zawahiri rejected the merger, creating a schism between the groups. Nevertheless, ISIS expanded its operations in northern and eastern Syria, claiming territory and creating tension with other rebel factions. The momentum allowed ISIS to attract additional resources, especially more foreign fighters.[24]

On New Year's Day 2014, ISIS convoys stormed Falluja and Ramadi, Iraqi cities which only a few years earlier had been liberated from extremists by U.S. forces. The Iraqi army crumbled as the fighters arrived in convoys of 70-100 trucks, armed with heavy weapons and anti-aircraft guns.[25] The group's growing success resonated with Islamist radicals across social media. ISIS launched another major offensive in June 2014, capturing Iraq's second largest city, Mosul, and taking control of others towns as it pushed south toward Baghdad.

The Declaration of the Caliphate and the Great Jihadi Migration

On June 29, 2014, ISIS declared it was re-establishing the "caliphate," or Islamic State, on the territory it controlled in Syria and Iraq.[26] Baghdadi was declared the State's leader—the caliph—via an audio recording posted online. In the eyes of ISIS followers, he was a successor to the prophet Muhammad and now the self-appointed leader of the Muslim world. ISIS called on Muslims to swear allegiance to the caliphate or be branded "apostates." Mainstream Muslims and even other jihadist groups dismissed the declaration as a stunt and declared the caliphate to be illegitimate.[27]

For many extremists, however, the announcement was groundbreaking. The establishment of an Islamic State had been the long-term goal of Osama bin Laden, though he did not believe it would happen in his lifetime. The declaration marked the first time in 90 years—since Turkish secularist Kemal Ataturk abolished the Ottoman Empire—that an Islamist group claimed dominion over the entire Muslim world.

A new wave of travelers headed to the region, aspiring to become jihadists and to participate in what they saw as a historic movement. Just days after the announcement, U.S. officials put the number of foreign fighters in Syria and Iraq at more than 7,000.[28] Within two months officials revised the figure upward to between 12,000 and 15,000.[29] The United Nations (UN) assessed militants from more than 80 countries had arrived.[30] The increase in numbers was partly from greater global awareness; as countries became more attuned to the threat, they realized more of their citizens traveled to the conflict zone and revised official figures accordingly. However, much of the growth was from new travelers.

ISIS militants started a new recruitment campaign to sell their society to a wider audience. The group promoted its territory as a place not just for fighters but also for families and called for extremists to bring their entire households— mothers, fathers and children—to the new Islamic State.[31] The group promised religious schooling for girls and boys and instruction for children on how to dress and maintain a household.[32] Women were promised homes with electricity, food, and salaries of up to $1,100 for each family—though they were likely not told the homes had come from locals who had been thrown out and the salaries looted from banks, oil smuggling, and kidnapping ransom.[11]

Despite using a softer pitch, the group's strongest appeal was to hardcore and aspiring extremists. ISIS promoted videos depicting its brutal murder of non-believers and sought to demonstrate its leadership of the global jihadist movement by intimidating Western countries. In August and September 2014, it released grisly videos of the beheading of several American, British, and Australian hostages.

Undeterred: Military Intervention and Continued Foreign Fighter Flows

The United States conducted its first series of coordinated airstrikes against ISIS in August 2014. The strikes focused initially on curbing ISIS advances in northern Iraq and protecting religious minorities but eventually shifted to supporting offensive operations against the militant group in both Iraq and its Syrian territory. In September, President Obama declared the aim of degrading and ultimately destroying the group. The United States has since conducted more than 5,000 airstrikes against ISIS.[14]

Airstrikes, however, do not appear to have kept aspiring foreign fighters away. When the strikes began, counterterrorism officials estimated the total number of extremists was around 15,000... Today the figure stands at 25,000-plus foreign fighters.

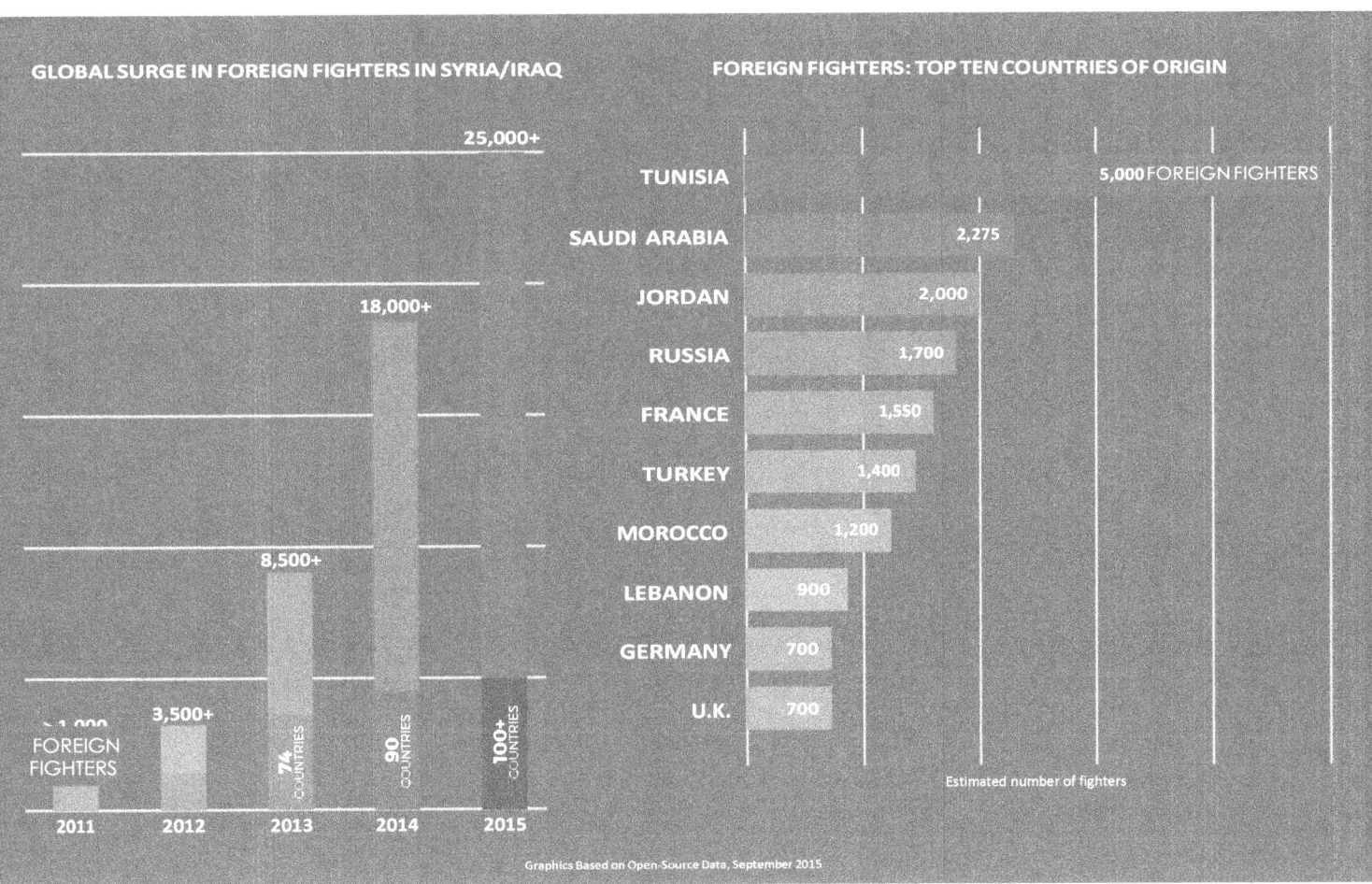

GLOBAL SURGE IN FOREIGN FIGHTERS IN SYRIA/IRAQ

25,000+

18,000+

8,500+

3,500+

~1,000
FOREIGN FIGHTERS

74 COUNTRIES

90 COUNTRIES

100+ COUNTRIES

2011   2012   2013   2014   2015

FOREIGN FIGHTERS: TOP TEN COUNTRIES OF ORIGIN

5,000 FOREIGN FIGHTERS

TUNISIA
SAUDI ARABIA   2,275
JORDAN   2,000
RUSSIA   1,700
FRANCE   1,550
TURKEY   1,400
MOROCCO   1,200
LEBANON   900
GERMANY   700
U.K.   700

Estimated number of fighters

Graphics Based on Open-Source Data, September 2015

Airstrikes, however, do not appear to have kept aspiring foreign fighters away. When the strikes began, counterterrorism officials estimated the total number of extremists was around 15,000.[35] However, fighters continued to enter Syria at a rate of about 1,000 per month. In December 2014, intelligence officials pegged the total at more than 18,000, [36] and by February 2015 it surpassed 20,000.[37] Today the figure stands at 25,000-plus foreign fighters, more than triple the number from just a year ago.[38] The majority of these fighters still come from the Middle East and North Africa, with Tunisia as the most significant source country. But the total also includes 4,500 Westerners and more than 250 Americans, figures which have surged since 2014.[39]

Indeed, foreign fighters have helped ISIS to remain strong. Nearly 10,000 of the group's foot soldiers have been killed by airstrikes, but they have been replaced by new foreign and domestic fighters almost as quickly as they are taken off the battlefield.[40] There has been "no meaningful degradation in their numbers," according to one defense official, as estimates place ISIS's total fighting force at 20-30,000—the same as it was last fall.[41]

New Sanctuaries

While ISIS is focused on holding its territory in Syria and Iraq, the group has also declared other "provinces" in places like Afghanistan, Algeria, Egypt, and Libya.[42] ISIS recruiters on social media have called for followers to travel to these locations if they cannot make it to Syria and Iraq, and it appears many have heeded the call. The groups has also publicly accepted pledges of allegiance from established Islamist terrorist groups like Boko Haram in Nigeria. Unlike al Qaeda, ISIS does not require a multiyear application process for groups to become a franchise of its terror brand, enabling it to grow faster and farther.[43]

Taking advantage of a post-Qaddafi security vacuum, ISIS has reportedly sent two senior foreign fighters to Libya to set up a new base of operations, and members of the group have put out recruitment calls for extremists to migrate there.[44] In early 2015, Libya's foreign minister estimated that more than 5,000 foreign fighters aligned with an array of terrorist groups had arrived in the country.[45] ISIS-linked militants trained in Libya are suspected of being responsible for devastating terrorist attacks in neighboring Tunisia, and officials fear the group may use Libya as a staging area to enter Europe by sea to attack Western countries.[46]

Foreign fighters pledging allegiance to ISIS have similarly been building a base of operations in Afghanistan and have been taking advantage of the Taliban's leadership vacuum to recruit additional fighters in the wake of its leader Mullah Omar's death. ISIS is reported to have amassed hundreds, if not thousands, of fighters in the country already.[47] Earlier this year Afghan President Ashraf Ghani warned of the "terrible threat" from the group, noting that it had "[sent] advance guards to southern and western Afghanistan to test for vulnerabilities."[48] ISIS now claims credit for terrorist attacks across Afghanistan.

While it is unclear whether any Western, or specifically American, foreign fighters have traveled to other ISIS terror sanctuaries, the group's expansion in these locations nevertheless provides a potential "menu" of options for jihadist travelers. Not only does this make it harder to roll back groups like ISIS, but it increases the challenges authorities face in tracking their own citizens who try to join the extremist movement.

The Danger of Foreign Fighters: Recruits, "Returnees," and Remote Radicalization

Foreign fighters represent a three-fold threat to the United States and the international community. First, they supply the human capital terrorist groups like ISIS need to operate, expand, and plot against the West. Second, "returnees" who come back from jihadist battlefields are often armed with the training to conduct attacks and the extremist connections to build terrorist networks at home. Third, even if fighters do not return home, they can engage others online from terror safe havens and inspire them to radicalize—or worse—to commit acts of violence without ever stepping foot out of the country.

Jihadists Without Borders

Foreign fighters have proven instrumental in fueling Islamist terror groups like ISIS. As noted earlier, jihadists from abroad have steadily backfilled the group's losses, preventing thousands of U.S. and coalition airstrikes from diminishing

> # We believe the hardest fighting people in ISIS are the foreign fighters. OFFICIAL TOLD TASK FORCE

its ranks. This of course has allowed ISIS to continue its reign of terror and even expand. Indeed, those who arrive in the conflict zone are typically willing and ready to participate in the group's atrocities. "We believe the hardest fighting people in ISIS are the foreign fighters," one official told the Task Force staff.[49]

Western recruits in particular have ended up at the forefront of the violence, and as one ISIS defector noted, they can be even more brutal than local jihadists.[50] Take the case of 26-year-old British citizen Mohammed Emwazi, better known as "Jihadi John." He is believed to have traveled to Syria around 2012 and to have later joined ISIS.[51] Before long, he had become the group's most visible spokesman and the masked face in its grisly beheading videos. After disappearing from public view for months, the British jihadist recently released a video pledging to return to Britain and "carry on cutting heads off."[52]

But Jihadi John is not an exception. Western foreign fighters have engaged heavily in the group's atrocities. Analysts for the International Center for the Study of Radicalization say extremists in Syria use Westerners for "excessively brutal operations that locals may refuse to be involved in," including suicide bombings, beheadings, and torture.[53] In fact, U.S. officials estimate most of the group's suicide bombers are from foreign countries.[54] One of the first Americans do die in the conflict, Moner Mohammad Abusalha, was responsible for a suicide bombing attack on a Syrian restaurant, the video of which was later distributed by extremists on social media.[55] In the recording, Abusalha rips up his American passport, urges others to travel to the conflict zone, and warns that America "is not safe"; it ends with him driving an explosive-laden truck into the attack site and detonating it.[56] In yet another indication Westerners are engaging in serious violence, Germany recently estimated that 100 of its 700 citizens who went to Syria had been killed while fighting alongside ISIS.[57]

> ## The biggest fear about those who travel to fight in terrorist hotspots is that they will return to plot attacks or to recruit others for their extremist networks.

The biggest fear about those who travel to fight in terrorist hotspots is that they will return to plot attacks or to recruit others for their extremist networks. A 2013 study found that one out of nine Western jihadists conducted attacks when they came back from conflict zones.[58] While this is only around 10 percent, it is still a worrying figure, given the fact that more than 25,000 extremists have gone abroad to become foreign fighters in Syria alone. Moreover, unlike many of the jihadists tracked in the study, today's extremists are more plugged into social media, allowing them to stay radicalized and engaged long after they have left the battlefield. Research also finds attacks conducted by returnees are more deadly than those carried out by homegrown extremists.[59]

These worries have materialized in the United States this year, as several American returnees have been arrested and charged by authorities.[60] In February, the FBI detained an Ohio man, Abdirahman Sheik Mohamud, who reportedly came back from training with extremists in Syria and planned to attack a U.S. military base and kill soldiers execution-style.[61] Mohamud returned after a radical, al Qaeda-affiliated cleric urged him to conduct an attack in the United States.[62] Another suspect, New York resident Arafat Nagi, was arrested in July and charged with attempting to recruit for ISIS after coming back from Turkey where he had sought to join the group.[63]

However, American returnees are not the only threat to the United States. Other Western citizens in the conflict zone—from dozens of countries—can travel easily to U.S. territory without applying for a visa, including most European jihadists.[64] European security officials estimate 20 to 30 percent of their foreign fighters have already departed Syria and Iraq.[65]

Since early 2014, there has been an alarming global uptick in terrorist plots involving foreign-fighter returnees. They include, but are not limited to, the following:[66]

- August 2015 (France): Plot to attack a concert on French soil; suspect allegedly returned from ISIS' stronghold in Raqqa, Syria with instructions to conduct the attack.[67]

- August 2015 (Belgium): Attempted mass shooting against passengers on a train from Amsterdam to Paris; suspect alleged to have fought in Syria.[68]

- July 2015 (Kosovo): Plot to contaminate the capital's water supply; two suspects believed to have fought in Syria.[69]

- June 2015 (Tunisia): Mass shooting on resort beach killing 40 people, mostly Western tourists; while suspect did not travel to Syria, he is said to have trained with ISIS in Libya.[70]

- April 2015 (Saudi Arabia): Plot to bomb U.S. Embassy in Riyadh; suspects include two Syrian foreign fighters and a Saudi citizen.[71]

- April 2015 (United States): Plot to attack a U.S. military base, as noted above; suspect trained in Syria and was directed to return to the United States to conduct attack.[72]

- March 2015 (United Kingdom): Plot to conduct mass public shooting; suspect was a British MI5 agent who had traveled to Syria and reportedly double-crossed his UK handlers.[73]

- March 2015 (Tunisia): Mass shooting attack killing 19 people at the National Bardo Museum in Tunis; two suspects allegedly trained in Libya with ISIS, which claimed credit for the attack.[74]

- March 2015 (Canada): Plot to bomb U.S. consulate in Canada; suspect who had allegedly trained with extremists in Pakistan and Libya.[75]

- January 2015 (Turkey): Plot to attack U.S., French, and Belgian consulates in Istanbul; suspects included 17 militants from Syria who infiltrated Turkey.[76]

- January 2015 (Belgium): Plot to conduct a major attack on police; two suspects killed during raid and had reportedly returned from Syria.[77]

- January 2015 (France): Shooting attack in Paris against cartoon publication; at least one suspect is believed to have returned from Yemen.

- May 2014 (Belgium): Shooting attack killing four at a Jewish museum in Brussels; suspect allegedly was ISIS militant in Syria.[78]

- February 2014 (France): Plot to bomb a carnival in the French Riviera; suspect had traveled to Syria to fight for ISIS.[79]

When they come back, foreign fighters are still a long-term threat no matter whether they engage in immediate attack plotting. Peter Neumann, a UK-based expert on the phenomenon, outlined the concerns clearly:

We don't know whether they will act today or tomorrow, but what we do know is that in five, 10, 15 years, not just next month, they will pose a danger. They've had military training; they've set up networks. We've seen it with the Afghan Arabs [i.e. the fighters who fought the Soviets in Afghanistan in the 1980s]. Many of them subsequently became involved in every conflict of the 1990s: Bosnia, Kosovo, Chechnya. Others went home to Libya, Pakistan, Afghanistan, and, once there, like the other Afghan Arabs, they became the elite: the leadership of the new jihad.[80]

PETER KEUMANN, UK-BASED EXPERT

Remote Radicalization

Even if foreign fighters do not return to the West, they still pose a threat by radicalizing others online. Most of the recruiting by groups like ISIS is not done through a central unit; it is performed at the grassroots by rank-and-file foreign fighters.[81] They have taken the lead in seeking new jihadist followers by communicating with others back home, documenting their battlefield experiences online, and distributing extremist propaganda on social media.

Many Islamist terror groups initially sought to recruit only men for the fighting. The approach has shifted, though, and groups like ISIS are encouraging women to migrate to its territory. Females who have made it to the conflict zone are now actively drafting other women. Umm Layth, a 20-year-old British citizen in Syria, for example, boasts a large social-media following and advises women on traveling to Syria, while others use Tumblr accounts to blog about daily ISIS life.[82]

Foreign jihadists have proven skilled at producing online content for each of their target audiences. Gruesome, Hollywood-style videos have been directed at recruiting potential martyrs and hardcore fighters. But ISIS has also sought to portray the lighter sides of its perceived caliphate to attract a wider following. The ninth issue of Dabiq, the group's online magazine, included a feature article on *"Healthcare in the [Caliphate],"* claiming ISIS provides "extensive healthcare by running a host of medical facilities including hospitals and clinics in all major cities."[83] The article adds that these facilities provide a "wide range of medical services," from x-rays and complex surgeries to ultrasounds and brain scans.[84] ISIS foreign fighters have also sought to appeal to those back home by emphasizing Western-style comforts. One social media campaign showed ISIS supporters posing with jars of Nutella,[85] while another documented the caliphate's ice cream parlors.[86]

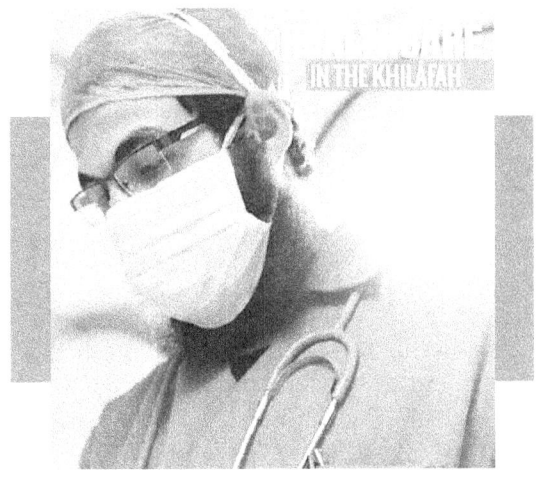

In addition to promoting travel to Syria and Iraq, foreign fighters also aim to radicalize Westerners back home to conduct attacks. For instance, authorities believe one of the shooters in the May assault on a draw-Mohammad contest in Garland, Texas was radicalized and directly encouraged online by a known ISIS recruiter in Syria.[87] This approach to supporting attacks—virtually reaching out to potential foot soldiers—has allowed the terror group to scale-up its violence. At the time of writing, there had been nearly twice as many ISIS-linked attack plots against the West in 2015 (37) as there were in all of 2014 (20).[88]

> There have now been more than twice as many ISIS-inspired terror plots against the West in 2015 than there were in all of 2014.

Intelligence officials estimate *more than 250 Americans* have tried or succeeded in getting to Syria and Iraq to fight with militant groups.[89] This includes individuals who were stopped before traveling, who made it to the conflict zone and are still there, who were killed, and others who have come back. Some have been arrested on terror charges, though most have not. Americans are being recruited in growing numbers and continue to attempt to migrate to jihadist battlefields in Syria and beyond, posing a serious counterterrorism challenge for the United States.

By-The-Numbers

The Task Force reviewed *58 cases of Americans* who joined or attempted to join Islamist terrorists in Syria and Iraq since the start of the Syrian civil war in 2011.[90] These individuals are listed in Appendix II. We did not review all American foreign fighter cases, only those which were publicly available. Some cases are not public due to ongoing investigations, while data about other suspects is often unconfirmed or classified.[91] Nevertheless, the instances we reviewed provide a sample of how widespread the foreign fighter phenomenon has become.

The majority of aspiring foreign fighters have managed to make it out of the United States without being stopped. Of the 250-plus Americans who have joined or tried to join extremists in Syria and Iraq, we were able to identify only 28 cases in which U.S. authorities apprehended suspects before they departed for the Middle East. A handful of suspects were stopped in other countries, but it appears the majority—more than 85 percent—still managed to evade American law enforcement on the way to the conflict zone. The first suspect authorities seem to have stopped was a 21-year-old Illinois man, Abdella Ahmad Tounsi, whose case is representative of many others. He was flagged after reaching out to an online terrorist recruiter, who was really an undercover FBI agent, and searching for ways to fight in Syria.[92] Tounsi was arrested in 2013 at O'Hare Airport where he planned to fly to Turkey and then travel into Syria to join al Qaeda's affiliate in the country.[93]

Airstrikes have not deterred radicalized Americans, who are attempting to travel to Syria at a growing rate. Based on the 58 cases we reviewed, there have been sharp increases in the number of Americans trying to travel to Syria each succeeding year (*10 percent of cases occurred in 2013, 40 percent in 2014,* and *50 percent in 2015*), indicating that coalition airstrikes in the region have not dissuaded travelers. Overall U.S. government figures confirm the growth: in late 2013, U.S. officials said "dozens" of Americans had sought to join Syrian rebels;[94] in July 2014, they estimated the figure to be around 100;[95] and by July of this year the estimates reached 250-plus.[96]

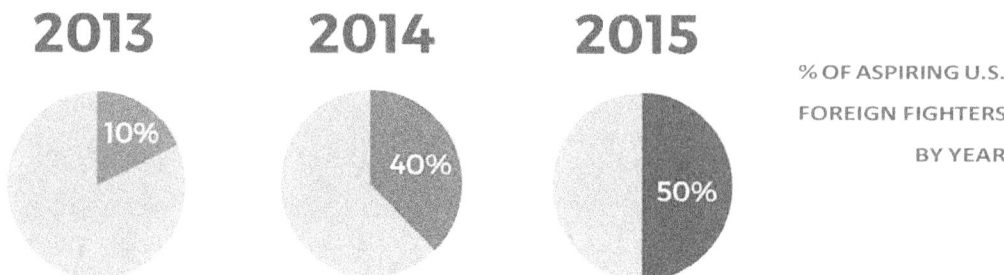

2013   2014   2015

10%   40%   50%

% OF ASPIRING U.S.
FOREIGN FIGHTERS
BY YEAR

Most aspiring fighters are now specifically attempting to join ISIS, not other terrorist groups. Early in the conflict, Americans were traveling to enlist with al Qaeda's affiliate in Syria, Jabhat al-Nusrah; around 20 percent of those we studied tried or succeeded in joining the group. However, the last known suspect traveled to join al-Nusra in early 2014; the other 80 percent sought to join ISIS. In March 2014, the FBI made its first arrest of an American trying to join ISIS when 20-year old community college student Nicholas Teausant was caught fleeing the country; the suspect had broadcast his extremist views widely on Facebook and Instagram before setting off for Syria.[97] Since then, many U.S. suspects have tread a common path: espousing their support for ISIS on social media and then attempting to leave America, en route to the so-called caliphate.

U.S. recruits are young and most are men. The average age of U.S. foreign fighters and aspirants in our sample was 24 years old, demonstrating jihadist groups are still primarily catering to a young audience. The youngest was 15 years old, while the oldest was 47. The majority we studied, 85 percent, were men. However, a growing number of women are being drawn to the conflict zone. Based on our sample, we estimate more than 30 American women have joined or attempted to join ISIS.[98]

Aspiring foreign fighters come from across America. We found young people from at least 19 U.S. states have sought to become foreign fighters in Syria and Iraq, with the most in our sample coming from Minnesota (26 percent), California (12 percent), and the New York / New Jersey area (12 percent).

Online propaganda and social media are major factors in U.S. recruitment. In almost 80 percent of cases, we found examples of U.S. foreign fighter aspirants downloading extremist propaganda, promoting it online, or engaging with other extremists on social media. Some communicated with ISIS fighters in Syria using secure messaging apps like Surespot or posed questions to overseas jihadists via the anonymous website Ask.fm; others promoted jihadist content across multiple platforms. Keonna Thomas, a Philadelphia mother who was arrested in April before attempting to leave the country, did both. She tweeted about becoming a martyr and responded eagerly to an ISIS fighter in Syria who messaged her about whether she would want to join a suicide operation. "That would be amazing," she responded. "A girl can only wish."[99]

Americans who make it to the conflict zone are reaching back to recruit others. A number of the cases we reviewed involved Americans who made it to Syria and attempted to remotely recruit others back home. Abdi Nur, only 20-years-old when he left Minnesota for Syria last year, is a prime example. Once in the conflict zone, he spent months persuading his friends in Minneapolis to join him. His peer-to-peer recruiting nearly worked, as six of his friends attempted to leave the United States for Syria; they were arrested by the FBI this April.[100] In a separate case, Ohio suspect Abdirahman Sheik Mohamud was urged by his brother Aden to join him overseas. Aden provided detailed instructions and contacts for getting from Turkey into the conflict zone.[101] Mohamud agreed to join him and left the United States for Syria, though his brother was later killed in the fighting.[102]

Roughly 20 percent of aspiring U.S. foreign fighters have been killed in Syria. Twelve of the 58 individuals we reviewed died after joining jihadist groups in the terrorist hotspot. Accordingly, we estimate nearly one in five Americans who have traveled or attempted to travel to Syria have been killed in the fighting. U.S. intelligence officials have already indicated more than 20 American have been killed.[103] Some reportedly died in fighting on the battlefield while others, like Florida resident Moner Abusalha, conducted suicide bombings.

Nearly all of those who have been apprehended are charged with "material support," but other charges have also been used. Ninety percent of arrested suspects have been charged with providing or attempting to provide "material support to a foreign terrorist organization"—usually in the form of trying to provide themselves as recruits to an extremist group. Several suspects have been arrested on charges of lying to authorities, passport fraud, gun crimes, or other infractions.

Around 10 percent of U.S. returnees have been arrested by authorities. Intelligence officials have indicated that around 40 Americans have returned from Syria after engaging with or pledging allegiance to jihadist groups, and our review found five of them have been arrested by authorities. Three were charged with providing material support to a foreign terrorist organization for allegedly engaging with al-Nusrah Front while in Syria; two others were charged with lying to the FBI, one of which had pledged allegiance to ISIS. One of the returnees was arrested plotting a terrorist attack against a U.S. military base.[104]

Human intelligence has been critical in stopping suspects. More than 75 percent of U.S. foreign-fighter arrest cases involved a confidential source, informant, family member, or concerned community member who cooperated with or tipped off authorities. In other words, private citizens have been key to detecting aspiring travelers. For example, in October 2014 three teenage girls from Denver attempted to join ISIS in Syria, but they were stopped when their parents alerted law enforcement.[105] The girls were detained in Germany and deported back to the United States.[106] In another case, several suspects were stopped in part because of a community member who changed his mind about joining ISIS and decided to cooperate with authorities.[107]

Peer-to-Peer Extremism: How Americans are Recruited Online and Lured Across Borders

Many past foreign-fighter cases involved individuals who were radicalized through personal contact with extremists, but that paradigm has changed. Based on our review, we find that the majority of U.S. foreign fighter aspirants were radicalized in part online, either through Islamist terror propaganda or peer-to-peer recruiting on social media. Indeed, as noted above, almost 80 percent of cases we studied involved radicalized Americans downloading extremist propaganda, promoting it online, or engaging with other extremists on Twitter, Facebook, and the like.

Recruits are motivated to join terrorist groups for a wide array of reasons. Many ISIS recruits, for instance, are inspired by jihadist ideology and see a historic opportunity to live in the caliphate. Others are motivated by the desire for adventure, to be a part of a cause larger than themselves, or for camaraderie and a sense of belonging. In almost all cases, though, suspects feel excluded from society or think they have failed to live up to expectations. These perceptions are often reinforced by a stressor life event, such as a drug arrest or school expulsion, that moves them to act. Other Americans aspired to travel to the terrorist safe haven believing they would find love, such as 19-year-old Shannon Maureen Conley, a nurse's aide from Colorado. She received a four-year prison sentence this year for attempting to join ISIS in Syria, where she planned to marry an ISIS fighter she met online.[108] Conley still reportedly signs her letters from jail with the closing "behind enemy lines."[109]

Online recruiters follow a similar path in trying to seduce Americans and other Westerners. They start by soliciting followers on social media, such as Twitter or Ask.fm, and "field questions about joining the Islamic State."[110] They then subtly proselytize to interested parties, providing "almost the online version of [a] religious seminar," observers note.[111] Once they spot promising extremists, recruiters will communicate with them using direct-message tools to determine whether they are serious and to weed out "spies."[112] Often extremists move the conversations to secure apps and encrypted platforms so they cannot be monitored while giving recruits instructions on traveling to Syria or even attack orders. FBI Director James Comey has equated the sophisticated outreach by ISIS recruiters to "a devil on their shoulder all day long saying, 'Kill, kill, kill.'"[113]

> One 23-year-old American woman reported that ISIS recruiters spent hours each day chatting with her. "I was on my own a lot, and they were online all the time."

One 23-year-old American woman reported that ISIS recruiters spent hours each day chatting with her.[114] "I was on my own a lot," she explained to The New York Times, "and they were online all the time."[115] One extremist in Syria with whom she communicated used methods consistent with a manual written by ISIS's predecessor, al Qaeda in Iraq: "A Course in the Art of Recruiting."[116] The manual recommends recruiters develop a relationship by keeping in regular touch with prospects, spending as much time with them as possible, listening to them carefully, and then drawing them closer to instill the basics of their ideology.[117] The woman's contacts spent months chatting with her, with one eventually urging her to travel to Syria.[118] The FBI reportedly interceded in the case, but several months later, the Times says the woman was still communicating online with extremists.[119]

Routes to the Conflict Zone: The "Jihadi Superhighway" and Beyond

Most American foreign fighters have traveled—or planned to travel—through Europe to get to Syria, according to the results of our review. The continent has become a "jihadi superhighway" to and from the conflict zone.[120] Turkey in particular has served as the primary point of entry and exit into Syria. In 55 percent of the cases we studied, suspects plotted to travel from America to Turkey, where they then planned to cross into Syria. The country's porous border has been an ideal gateway for aspiring jihadists seeking to get in and out of the terrorist safe haven.

> I just went online and bought a ticket. It was that easy. It was like booking a flight to Miami Beach.
> AMERICAN WHO WENT TO FRONTLINES IN SYRIA

While Turkey has begun to crack down on illegal border crossings, foreign fighter flows appear to continue unabated.[121] "This is an easy battlefield to get to," an

PEER-to-PEER TERRORIST RECRUITING

1 OPEN-SOURCE "CALL TO ARMS"

Using Twitter, Facebook, YouTube, and other public forms of social media to *identify* recruits and give general advice.

2 SHIFT TO PRIVATE COMMUNICATIONS

Using email, direct Facebook or Twitter messages, or messaging apps such as WhatsApp to *assess and develop* recruits.

3 "GOING DARK"

Using the deep web or encrypted messaging services like Wickr and Surespot to *plot attacks or plan travel to overseas terrorist hotspots.*

Administration official conceded to the Task Force.[122] One American who traveled to Syria and fought on the frontlines with rebels echoed the assessment. "I just went online and bought a ticket," he explained. "It was that easy. It was like booking a flight to Miami Beach."[123]

Foreign-fighter recruiters have tried to make it simple for Americans to join them abroad. Supporters distribute manuals providing plain, English-language advice on getting to the safe haven. In February 2015, ISIS published "Hijrah to the Islamic State," a how-to guide for dealing with border security, planning travel routes, and deciding what to pack.[124] Another manual, "How to Survive in the West," advises followers on avoiding law enforcement detection and instructs them on getting in touch with extremists once they arrive.[125] FBI Assistant Director Michael Steinbach said in a February hearing that the support individuals receive as they prepare to migrate to the conflict zone has been tough to combat. The problem is "not even close to being under control," he explained.[126]

Extremists are also advising travelers to "break" their

travel to make it more difficult for authorities to catch them.[127] ISIS recruiters are urging followers to buy airline tickets to holiday destinations that do not look suspicious and, once there, book onward travel to Turkey.[128] Would-be fighters are also using what is popularly known as "hidden city ticketing" by booking a flight to a false end-destination and getting off the plane at the connecting stop. One of the Americans who made it to Syria used this tactic. He bought a one-way flight to Greece with a connection in Istanbul. According to the indictment, he never boarded his connecting flight and instead made his way to the battlefield.[129]

Extremists on no-fly lists or seeking to avoid law enforcement scrutiny at airports have opted instead to travel by land or sea. Most commonly, these aspiring fighters have driven or taken buses through the Balkans to the Bulgarian or Greek border, where they then enter Turkey.[130] Alternatively, extremists have found they can board Turkey-bound ferries and cruise ships from Mediterranean countries, where there is little security and passports are often not checked.[131]

KEY FINDINGS & RECOMMENDATIONS

The Task Force makes **32 Key Findings** and associated recommendations to improve America's security posture—and to ensure foreign countries are doing the same. Below is an abbreviated summary with references to the appropriate sections where complete descriptions of each Key Finding can be found.

U.S. Government Strategy and Planning to Combat the Threat

Key Finding 1: The U.S. lacks a comprehensive strategy for combating terrorist and foreign fighter travel. **p. 22**

Key Finding 2: Despite concerted efforts to stem the flow, we have largely failed to stop Americans from traveling overseas to join jihadists. **p. 23**

Key Finding 3: The growing complexity of the threat may be creating unseen gaps in our defenses, yet it has been years since any large-scale "stress test" has been conducted on U.S. defenses against terrorist travel. **p. 23**

Key Finding 4: ISIS operatives are urging followers to travel to the group's other "provinces" in places like Libya, yet it is unclear whether agencies are keeping pace with changes in foreign-fighter destinations. **p. 24**

Key Finding 5: Ultimately, severing foreign fighter flows depends on eliminating the problem at the source. **p. 24**

Identifying Terrorists and Foreign Fighters—and Preventing Them from Traveling

Key Finding 6: Improvements have been made to the terrorist watchlisting process, yet no independent review has been done to assess them and whether more are needed in light of the evolving threat environment. **p. 26**

Key Finding 7: Individuals can now contest their status on the no-fly list; however, more should be done to ensure the new process will appropriately balance due process rights with national security concerns. **p. 27**

Key Finding 8: Despite improvements since 9/11, foreign partners are still sharing information about terrorist suspects in a manner which is ad hoc, intermittent, and often incomplete. **p. 28**

Key Finding 9: There is currently no comprehensive global database of foreign fighter names. Instead, countries including the U.S. rely on a weak, patchwork system for swapping individual extremist identities. **p. 29**

Key Finding 10: DHS should continue its efforts to quickly leverage unclassified data in classified environments to identify potential foreign fighters. **p. 30**

Key Finding 11: The DHS Counterterrorism Advisory Board has not been authorized by Congress nor does its charter reflect recent changes to the threat environment, including the rise of the foreign fighter threat. **p. 30**

Key Finding 12: More can be done to incorporate valuable "financial intelligence" into counterterrorism screening and vetting processes. **p. 31**

Key Finding 13: State and local fusion centers are underutilized by federal law enforcement nationwide when it comes to combating the immediate foreign fighter threat and terrorist travel generally. **p. 32**

Key Finding 14: State and local law enforcement personnel continue to express concern that they are not provided with the appropriate security clearances to assist with counterterrorism challenges. **p. 32**

Key Finding 15: The unprecedented speed at which Americans are being radicalized by violent extremists is straining federal law enforcement's ability to monitor and intercept suspects before it's too late. **p. 33**

Key Finding 16: Few initiatives exist nationwide to raise community awareness about foreign-fighter recruitment and to assist communities with spotting warning signs. **p. 33**

Key Finding 17: The federal government has failed to develop clear intervention strategies—or "off-ramps" to radicalization—to prevent suspects already on law enforcement's radar from leaving to join extremists. **p. 34**

Key Finding 18: Jihadist recruiters are increasingly using secure websites and apps to communicate with Americans, making it harder for law enforcement to disrupt plots and terrorist travel. **p. 35**

Key Finding 19: The Administration has launched programs to counter-message terrorist propaganda abroad, but little is being done here at home.   **p. 36**

Key Finding 20: The U.S. has not made adequate use of "jaded jihadists" to convince others not to join the fight. **p. 37**

Key Finding 21: Unlike many other governments, U.S. authorities have not relied heavily on passport revocation to stop extremists. **p. 37**

Detecting and Disrupting Terrorists and Foreign Fighters When They Travel

Key Finding 22: While substantial progress has been made since 9/11 to enhance visa security, there may be additional opportunities to expand screening to identify potential extremists earlier in the process. **p. 39**

Key Finding 23: The Administration has improved the security of the Visa Waiver Program, but continuous enhancements must be made in light of the changing threat. **p. 40**

Key Finding 24: U.S. authorities remain concerned about terrorists posing as refugees, yet it is unclear to what extent security improvements to the refugee screening process mitigate potential vulnerabilities. **p. 42**

Key Finding 25: "Broken travel" and other evasive tactics are making it harder to track foreign fighters. **p. 43**

Key Finding 26: More could be done to give frontline operators at borders and ports better intelligence reach-back capabilities so DHS can "connect the dots" and uncover previously unidentified terrorists and foreign fighters. **p. 44**

Key Finding 27: U.S. authorities continue to "push the border outward" by deploying homeland security initiatives overseas. Expanding these efforts might help detect threats sooner. **p. 44**

Key Finding 28: Only a fraction of U.S. states have access to INTERPOL databases; wider access could help spot wanted foreign fighters who have slipped past border security.   **p. 45**

Overseas Security Gaps

Key Finding 29: Gaping security weaknesses overseas—especially in Europe—are putting the U.S. homeland in danger by making it easier for aspiring foreign fighters to migrate to terrorist hotspots and for jihadists to return to the West. **p. 46**

Key Finding 30: Extremists are using fraudulent passports to travel discretely. However, a third of the international community—including major source countries of foreign fighters—still do not issue fraud-resistant "e-passports," and most countries are still unable to validate the authenticity of "e-passports."   **p. 52**

Key Finding 31: Many countries do not consistently add information to INTERPOL's databases, and the majority do not screen against INTERPOL databases in real-time at their borders and airports. **p. 53**

Key Finding 32: U.S. departments and agencies have spent billions of dollars to help foreign partners improve their terror-travel defenses, but the lack of a coordinated strategy for such assistance results in greater risk of overlap, waste, and duplication between programs. **p. 54**

U.S. GOVERNMENT STRATEGY & PLANNING

After the attacks of September 11, 2001, it was clear America needed to take urgent steps to keep terrorists from entering its borders. The 9/11 Commission, for instance, found it was so easy for the hijackers to operate within the United States that they traveled "into, out of, and around the country and complacently [used] their real names with little fear of capture."[132] Since then, the U.S. government has taken extraordinary steps to disrupt terrorists at all stages of travel—from fusing real-time intelligence into the border screening process to enhancing travel-document security. These measures have made it harder for extremists to cross our borders.

But the threat environment has evolved, which is why the Task Force conducted its review. While post-9/11 reforms focused largely on preventing terrorists from infiltrating our country to attack, today we need to be equally concerned about keeping Americans from exiting our country to join terrorist groups. The latter challenge demands a different set of tools. This is why it is important for the government to be able to adjust its strategies and plans. We must adapt to new threats and get resources where they are needed.

Unfortunately, our country has a surplus of programs for combating terrorist travel but a deficit of strategic guidance to keep them aligned with the threat. Agencies must be able to make sense of new trends, take stock of existing counterterrorism efforts, and pivot to fix weaknesses. Yet the Task Force found there is no clear, whole-of-government system for cataloging the proliferation of terror-travel programs, nor a strategy to "stitch the seams" between them.

The Administration has undoubtedly stepped up security to cut off foreign fighter flows, as documented throughout this report, but more must be done to identify and close potential gaps in our defenses against terrorist travel writ large.

Key Finding 1: *The U.S. government lacks a comprehensive strategy for combating terrorist and foreign fighter travel and has failed to maintain a system for identifying and plugging related gaps in America's defenses.*

It has been nearly a decade since the Executive Branch produced a whole-of-government plan to constrain terrorist movements. In its 2004 final report, the 9/11 Commission recommended the United States develop "a strategy to intercept terrorists, find terrorist travel facilitators, and constrain terrorist mobility." That year, Congress passed the Intelligence Reform and Terrorism Prevent Act, which mandated such a plan, required the Administration to explain how it would be implemented, and called for an assessment of vulnerabilities in U.S. and foreign travel systems that could be exploited by extremists.[133] The result was the 2006 National Strategy to Combat Terrorist Travel.[134] It has not been updated since.

The 2006 Strategy is woefully outdated. While it provided a thorough overview of U.S. efforts to keep extremists from crossing borders, some of those programs have changed or are now defunct, and new ones have been created. The evolving threat environment has also made the document obsolete. For instance, the Strategy makes no mention of foreign fighters or the challenges associated with extremists' social media recruiting.

There appears to be no comprehensive accounting of terrorist-travel programs in the U.S. government or any systematic government-wide efforts to identify gaps between them. The President's 2011 National Strategy for Counterterrorism makes little mention of the subject aside from noting the United States will work with foreign partners to "identify terrorist operatives and prevent their travel...across national borders and within states."[135] A full audit of America's terror-travel preventative and protective measures should be produced, as the Administration has identified "disrupting the flow of foreign fighters" as one of its top priorities in the fight against ISIS.[136]

We found that hundreds of programs, projects, and initiatives have sprouted up to combat terrorist travel since 9/11, but without an overarching strategy to coordinate them, the United States may be wasting taxpayer dollars and failing to allocate resources where they are needed most. Indeed, lack of a strategy not only increases the risk terrorists might exploit weaknesses in the U.S. travel system, but also raises the prospect of waste, overlap, and duplication between agencies.

Recommendation: The Executive Branch should provide a National Strategy to Combat Terrorist Travel to Congress. Thereafter, the Administration should annually assess the evolving terror threat to the United States, catalogue existing U.S. government programs designed to obstruct terrorist travel, propose areas for reform and the elimination of duplicative programs, identify gaps in our defenses, and prioritize resources to fill gaps in a risk-based fashion. The strategy should not only take into account the travel into the United States of known or suspected terrorists but should also consider foreign fighter travel to terrorist safe havens.

Key Finding 2: *Despite concerted efforts to stem the flow, we have largely failed to stop Americans from traveling overseas to join jihadists. Of the hundreds of Americans who have sought to travel to the conflict zone in Syria and Iraq, authorities have only interdicted a fraction of them. Several dozen have also managed to make it back into America.*

Around 40 American foreign fighters have made it back to the United States, and some individuals have gone back and forth to the conflict zone multiple times.

The Task Force was only able to identify 28 cases where U.S. individuals were stopped before leaving the United States—a small fraction of the total that have attempted to travel to the conflict zone.[117] A handful of others were stopped at other stages of the journey. The majority appear to have succeeded, despite concerted government efforts to prevent Americans from joining groups like ISIS abroad. In fact, around 40 have even made it back to the United States, and some individuals have gone back and forth to the conflict zone multiple times.[118] One suspect from Florida allegedly trained with extremists in Syria and returned to the United States for several months before heading back to the conflict zone; during that time, he was never on the radar screen of U.S. authorities.[119]

We believe it is unacceptable that so many Americans have been able to make it to the world's most dangerous terrorist safe haven (and back) without being interdicted. While we commend the FBI, the Department of Homeland Security (DHS), and other agencies for a string of successful arrests this year, a great deal can and must be learned from instances where we failed, including what was known and when about each suspect and whether more could have been done to stop them. This may help reveal any systemic weaknesses in the security architecture we have built into the U.S. travel system since 9/11.

Unfortunately, the Administration has not called for a formal government-wide examination of these cases. Some agencies have done their own "after action" reviews which have produced useful conclusions, but there is yet to be a coordinated and comprehensive interagency investigation into why each of these Americans slipped through the cracks. Our Task Force has identified some of the security weaknesses highlighted by the foreign fighter phenomenon, but only the Executive Branch has the time and resources to do the comprehensive, deep-dive review that is needed of all of the recent American foreign fighter cases.

Recommendation: The Administration should launch an end-to-end review of all cases involving Americans traveling or attempting to travel to Syria and Iraq to join Islamist terror groups—taking into consideration all relevant classified and unclassified information—to determine what lessons can be learned and to prevent additional Americans from traveling to overseas terrorist sanctuaries. The final conclusions should be presented to Congress, along with any relevant legislative recommendations.

Key Finding 3: *The growing complexity and changing nature of the foreign fighter phenomenon may be creating unseen gaps in our defenses, yet it has been years since any large-scale "stress test" has been conducted on U.S. government protection and prevention programs against terrorist travel.*

The last major government exercise on terrorist travel occurred in 2009. That year, the Federal Emergency Management Agency (FEMA) managed an exercise centered on the "aftermath of a notional terrorist event outside of the United States" and how to prevent "subsequent efforts by the terrorists to enter the United States and carry out additional attacks."[140] The exercise tested how agencies at all levels of government would respond in such a scenario.

But the threat environment has changed. The 2009 exercise centered on terrorists attempting to enter the country, but as we have noted, officials today should be just as concerned about Americans leaving the country to train overseas with terrorist groups as foreign fighters. Such individuals can represent a serious security threat to the United States, particularly upon their return to the country, so preventing them from joining extremists abroad in the first place should be a top law enforcement goal.

> **Recommendation:** The White House should lead a national-level exercise series designed around the foreign fighter threat to test all phases of extremist planning and travel to determine how partners at all levels of government—and abroad—are currently responding to these scenarios. The primary focus of the exercises should be to identify weaknesses at home and abroad that may be exploited by terrorists and foreign fighters seeking to travel to and from the United States and overseas terrorist sanctuaries.[141]

Key Finding 4: *In addition to Syria and Iraq, ISIS operatives are urging followers to travel to the group's other "provinces" in places like Libya, yet it is unclear to what extent departments and agencies are shifting diplomatic, intelligence, law enforcement, policy, and other resources to keep pace with and track evolving foreign fighter flows to other emerging safe havens.*

ISIS continues to boast to its followers that it has expanded beyond Syria and Iraq. Indeed, the group now has a direct presence, affiliates, or groups pledging support in at least 18 countries or territories, including: Afghanistan, Algeria, Egypt, India, Indonesia, Iraq, Jordan, Libya, Lebanon, Nigeria, the Palestinian territories, Pakistan, the Philippines, Russia (North Caucasus region), Sudan, Syria, Tunisia, and Yemen.[142] The ability for extremists to operate openly in many of these areas is tenuous, but several are emerging terrorist sanctuaries.

ISIS operatives have urged followers on social media to head to its other provinces. In one online handbook popular with extremists, the author writes that "if the Muslim finds it hard to flee to the Islamic State in Iraq and Syria through Turkey, he can escape to the Islamic State in Libya, or [Afghanistan/Pakistan], or in Nigeria (under Boko Haram territory)."[143] Thousands of foreign fighters appear to be heeding the call in places like Libya, and others have reportedly begun to appear in Nigeria.[144] It is unclear if there are Westerners in these groups, but the trend is disturbing.

Current U.S. government efforts to combat the flow of foreign fighters are heavily focused on keeping fighters from traveling to and from Syria and Iraq, but as we have seen, the terror threat environment can change quickly. Radicalized individuals who were once intent on traveling to Afghanistan or Somalia are now traveling to Syria, and more may soon begin traveling to new ISIS outposts. We cannot be caught off guard by changes in terror-travel destinations, which is why law enforcement and the intelligence community must continue to closely track changes in extremist migration to new terrorist hot spots.

> **Recommendation:** The Intelligence Community should provide Congress with regular updates documenting foreign fighter flows to other terrorist sanctuaries, in addition to Syria and Iraq, and in coordination with interagency partners should provide updates on actions being taken to prevent extremist migration to those locations.

Key Finding 5: *Ultimately, severing foreign fighter flows to any conflict zone depends on eliminating the problem at the source and preventing the emergence of terrorist sanctuaries.*

We are playing defense over here, but what we are doing overseas—the offense—is key.

SENIOR OFFICAL TOLD TASK FORCE

We find that, in the long run, the only truly effective method for preventing our citizens from joining terrorist organizations abroad is to eliminate the sanctuaries in which those groups thrive. "We are playing defense over here," one senior official told the Task Force, "but what we are doing overseas—the offense—is key."[145]

The "center of gravity" of the current foreign fighter phenomenon is still in Syria and Iraq, and as long as the safe haven in that region persists, so will the drive of individuals around the world—including radicalized Americans—to migrate to it. Indeed, the safe haven enhances the perceived legitimacy of groups like ISIS, helping to radicalize even more individuals to its cause.

Terrorist groups thrive in the world's lawless outposts. We have learned this the hard way. If left unaddressed, failing states and ungoverned spaces become the playgrounds of fanatics, who exploit these areas to expand their influence, solicit recruits, and plot attacks. We have seen this in Syria. We have seen this in Afghanistan. And we have seen this in the Arabian Peninsula and the Horn of Africa. Without clear strategies to identify and prevent the emergence of extremist sanctuaries, America risks those locations becoming new headquarters of terrorist planning against our homeland.

"Every policy decision we make needs to be seen through this lens," the 9/11 Commission wrote more than a decade ago. The Commission offered the following warning: "If, for example, Iraq becomes a failed state, it will go to the top of the list of places that are breeding grounds for attacks against Americans at home. Similarly, if we are paying insufficient attention to Afghanistan...its countryside could once again offer refuge to al Qaeda, or its successor."[146]

Recommendation: In the near term, the United States and its allies must defeat terrorist groups in Syria and Iraq to

> keep Westerners from being drawn to the region where they are further radicalized and trained by violent extremists. In the long run, the U.S. government must heed the advice of the 9/11 Commission and "identify and prioritize actual or potential terrorist sanctuaries" and develop realistic strategies to prevent extremists from taking root within them.
>
> An effective counterterrorism system must be able to recognize extremist suspects in order to prevent them

IDENTIFICATION & PREVENTION

from crossing borders, and if they do, authorities must be alerted to their movements so they can be stopped. Accordingly, the Task Force categorized four phases critical for stopping terrorist and foreign fighter travel: (1) identification, (2) prevention, (3) detection, and (4) disruption. Information sharing is a critical pillar of the identification phase. From state and local police to foreign governments, intelligence must be disseminated quickly and securely to ensure frontline operators are able to spot violent extremists. More robust terrorism watchlists, for instance, have allowed U.S. authorities to keep thousands of potentially dangerous individuals with terrorist ties out of the United States since 9/11.

However, preventing individuals from traveling out of the country to terrorist safe havens remains a difficult task. In many cases, intelligence agencies and police are unaware of an American's plan to travel overseas to link up with terrorists until after he or she has already left. When authorities are made aware, in many cases it is because of a tip from family, friends, or community members. Even then, preventing a suspect's travel can be difficult. The Task Force examined America's progress in the "identification and prevention" phases of terrorist and foreign fighter travel, and we propose a number of urgent improvements to strengthen our country's defenses.

Watchlisting

The 9/11 Commission found that before the 2001 terrorist attacks, the United States lacked a single list of suspected terrorists and did not distribute a similar document or database to relevant departments and agencies.[147] This meant even terrorist known to authorities might be able to evade screening systems at the border. After 2001, the White House and Congress mandated the creation an integrated terrorist watchlist and required agencies to better fuse intelligence information into it.

The result is that today America boasts the most sophisticated watchlisting and screening system in the world. Authorities have gone to great lengths to integrate intelligence databases into a centralized clearinghouse of terrorist suspects, which is then used to compile the terrorist watchlist, known officially as the Terrorist Screening Database (TSDB). The TSDB is one of our most effective tools for detecting the movement of extremists. For instance, agencies like the Transportation Security Administration (TSA), FBI, and state and local law enforcement rely on the watchlist to identify known or suspected terrorists trying to board aircraft, obtain visas, enter the country, or engage in other activities.[148]

Key Finding 6: *Both the 2009 Christmas Day bombing of a U.S. airliner and the 2013 Boston Marathon Bombing led to extensive improvements in the terrorist watchlisting process. Yet no independent review has been conducted to assess the impact of recent changes to the watchlisting process and whether further changes are warranted in light of the evolving threat environment.*

TERRORIST WATCHLISTING PROCESS

STEP 1

Information is collected about known / suspected international and domestic terrorists

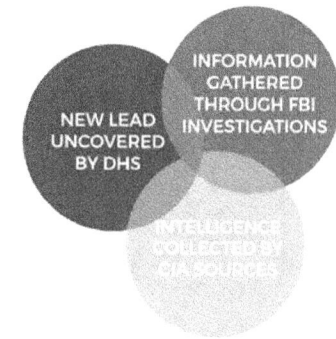

INFORMATION GATHERED THROUGH FBI INVESTIGATIONS

NEW LEAD UNCOVERED BY DHS

INTELLIGENCE COLLECTED BY CIA SOURCES

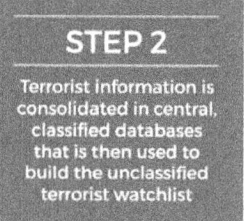

STEP 2

Terrorist information is consolidated in central, classified databases that is then used to build the unclassified terrorist watchlist

TIDE DATABASE
(managed by the NCTC)

LIST

TERRORIST WATCHLIST
(managed by FBI's Terror Screening Center)

STEP 3

Agencies use the consolidated watchlist to detect known or suspected terrorists

EXAMPLE

Passengers screened before entering the United States

On Christmas Day 2009, Nigerian citizen Umar Farouk Abdulmutallab—known widely as the "underwear bomber"—attempted to detonate explosives on Northwest Airlines Flight 253. A subsequent White House review determined that counterterrorism agencies had information that raised red flags about Abdulmutallab but failed to connect the dots and place him on the terrorist watchlist.[149] Doing so may have prevented him from boarding the aircraft and may have resulted in additional screening that could have detected his explosives.

Similarly, following the 2013 Boston Marathon Bombing, authorities determined that information held by the U.S. government about Tamerlan Tsarnaev was not pieced together comprehensively. A fully consolidated and accurate record for Tsarnaev in the terrorist watchlist might have led authorities to perform additional screening when he returned from Russia, where he is alleged to have met with Islamist militants.[150]

The National Counterterrorism Center (NCTC) and the interagency community have made commendable progress in recent years to close gaps in the watchlisting process, to ensure critical intelligence information is integrated in near-real-time to our screening systems, and to make sure data from disparate sources is combined to better identify extremists. Multiple revisions to the interagency Watchlisting Guidance have been made in recent years, resulting in a larger (but more accurate) terrorist watchlist. Improvements have also led to an array of interagency initiatives to ensure authorities on the frontlines have the timely information they need to stop terrorist movements.

Nevertheless, no independent review has been conducted of these changes to the watchlisting and screening process. In 2012, the Government Accountability Office (GAO) recommended regular assessments of the watchlisting process were warranted to ensure the watchlist is achieving its intended outcomes.[151] Interagency policy reviews have been conducted of this critical counterterrorism tool, but we believe it is important for a third-party to ensure security deficiencies have been fixed and that policies and procedures are keeping pace with an evolving threat environment—especially the threat from foreign fighters.

> **Recommendation:** GAO should conduct an independent review to determine whether past weaknesses in the watchlisting process have been reconciled and whether additional changes are needed to enhance America's defenses. This includes ensuring that information is being integrated into the terrorist watchlist from all relevant sources across the government, that it is being done in a timely manner, that agencies are equipped to handle increased demands for information to improve the watchlist, that the right authorities have the watchlist access they need, and that individuals who should no longer be included on the list are removed appropriately.

Key Finding 7: *The Administration has revised the administrative "redress" process, which allows an individual who has purchased a plane ticket, been denied boarding, and sought redress, to contest his or her inclusion on the no-fly list; however, more work should be done to ensure that judicial review of such listings appropriately balances due process rights with national security concerns.*

In connection with a number of court cases pending across the country where individuals challenged their inclusion on the no-fly list, DHS has made significant changes to the redress process by which such listings are reviewed. Among other things, U.S. persons who purchase a ticket, are denied boarding, and subsequently seek to challenge an alleged no-fly listing, are now informed as to whether they are on the list and, if they are on the list, given an opportunity to request additional information. If the individual seeks additional information, DHS then provides a second, more detailed response, which will include the applicable no-fly criterion and, where possible, additional unclassified information. This change allows affected Americans to have access to more information with which to respond through the administrative process.

However, issues remain if these matters proceed to courts. Departments and agencies claim there are major challenges in the court system with appropriately handling the classified, privileged, or sensitive information on which no-fly listings are often based. Current law does not provide a statutory mechanism for addressing these issues, and as a result, some cases may not be able to be decided on the merits. We need a system that enables judicial review of no-fly list decisions based on the facts and with respect to individual rights, while also establishing effective mechanisms for the protection of classified or otherwise sensitive information.

Recommendation: The Administration should provide Congress with a formal plan for reforming the process for review of no-fly listings which safeguards civil liberties, due process, and national security in line with recent court decisions. This plan should include any legislative changes sought by the Administration to ensure classified or otherwise sensitive information is handled appropriately and protected from disclosure when no-fly listings are challenged in court.

Information Sharing

It is difficult to overstate how important post-9/11 information sharing has been in combating terrorist threats to the United States. American lives have been saved and our country is safer because of tectonic shifts in the level of cooperation between agencies at home and with foreign partners. When it comes to disrupting terrorist travel, information sharing is the backbone of a strong security posture. If one agency identifies a violent extremist and fails to notify other partners, the suspect may easily enter our country undetected. That is why at all levels of government (international, federal, State, and local) the exchange of terrorist identities has become a leading national security objective.

The foreign fighter threat—whether from Americans seeking to join terrorists abroad or returning home from extremist safe havens—presents challenges to our information-sharing environment. The sheer volume of jihadist travelers has made it difficult for authorities to keep track of individuals who pose a threat and turn attention away from those who do not. In response, the Administration has taken action to ramp up information-sharing activities, from improving intelligence exchanges with our allies to sending more frequent bulletins to state and local law enforcement.

We believe even more can be done to ensure federal, state, and local agencies are quickly exchanging information about suspects in an environment where radicalization happens far more quickly than ever before. And we believe more must be done abroad. Foreign partner information sharing is uneven, leading to gaps in our collective knowledge of the individuals who have traveled to dangerous terrorist sanctuaries.

Key Finding 8: *America relies on foreign partner intelligence information to identify terrorists and foreign fighters, yet many countries still share the names of suspects with the United States in a manner that is ad hoc, intermittent, and often incomplete—a worrying gap in our defenses against extremist travel.*

Foreign fighters can only be stopped from crossing borders (and prevented from conducting attacks) if authorities are aware of them. This means countries must share fighter names with the United States so those individuals can be appropriately watchlisted. Sharing has improved with our partners lately, but there are still disturbing weaknesses. For example, European security services reportedly failed to share the name of a suspected extremist who returned from Syria and attempted a mass shooting in August on a train from Amsterdam to Paris, even though the assailant was on the radar of European authorities.[152] If the suspect had attempted instead to travel to America to conduct the attack, U.S. authorities likely would not have noticed since the individual was not on our watchlist. That is why information sharing is so important.

In 2003, President Bush issued Homeland Security Presidential Directive 6 (HSPD-6), which directed U.S. agencies to work with foreign governments to exchange terrorist screening information, particularly the names and identifiers of known or suspected terrorists. The United States has since signed agreements with more than 40 countries to swap terrorist watchlist data, including most Visa Waiver Program (VWP) countries. Although the United States also shares such data through other channels, HSPD-6 agreements are seen as enhancing the transparency, frequency, and quality of those exchanges.

However, information-sharing among many of the countries who have signed HSPD-6 pacts remains inadequate. Some countries signed agreements years ago, but have never used the mechanism to share terrorist names with the United States or do so only infrequently.[153] Moreover, while some are willing to share the names of suspected terrorists and foreign fighters, others are reportedly only willing to share the identities of convicted terrorists.[154] This creates potentially disturbing gaps in our awareness of extremists who may attempt travel to the United States.

Some countries are also reluctant to share names of their own citizens for privacy reasons, even if those individuals are terror suspects they are tracking. In these cases, foreign partners will presumably share a name if the suspect tries to travel to the United States. But in places like Europe where there are few internal border checkpoints, it is difficult to see how authorities would know if their citizens were headed to America. A German suspect could easily drive to Spain, for instance, to evade German authorities and fly to America undetected.

It is also unclear to what extent foreign partners are reporting all of the "encounters" they have with terrorists from our own watchlists that we have warned them about. While some HSPD-6 countries let U.S. authorities know when they have run into individuals we have flagged, they are not necessarily required to do so in real-time or to provide details of those encounters. Moreover, there still appears to be no universal case management system for foreign partners to report when they have encountered a suspect from our watchlist.[155]

Senior officials have acknowledged to the Task Force that until recently, the United States has rarely put serious pressure on our foreign partners to live up to their HSPD-6 agreements. Only with the rise in the foreign fighter threat did U.S. departments and agencies begin to push foreign partners to share names more regularly and thoroughly using the process. Sharing reportedly has improved, but there is clearly more to be done to increase participation and accountability.

> **Recommendation:** The Inspectors General of DHS, the State Department, the FBI, and the Intelligence Community should conduct a deep-dive review of the U.S. government's HSPD-6 information-sharing agreements, the process for reaching and enforcing agreements, compliance with such agreements, possible performance indicators, and related matters to determine if more can be done to standardize, streamline, and enhance foreign fighter information sharing with partners. The review should be provided to Congress.

> **Recommendation:** DHS, FBI, and the State Department should provide a classified report annually to Congress on HSPD-6 information-sharing agreements and compliance, by country. The Administration should also provide Congress with any proposals to adjust the requirements of HSPD-6 information sharing agreements and to increase foreign partner compliance.

> **Recommendation:** GAO should complete its ongoing review of the overall status of information-sharing agreements required under the VWP and provide Congress with an overview of any identified weaknesses or concerns.

Key Finding 9: *There is currently no comprehensive global database of foreign fighter names. Instead, countries including the United States rely on a patchwork system for swapping individual extremist identities. This is an inherently weak arrangement that increases the odds a foreign fighter will be able to cross border undetected when traveling to and from a terrorist sanctuary.*

Countries around the globe continue to rely on bilateral and regional information-sharing agreements to exchange terrorist watchlists and compare foreign fighter names. The result is that global awareness of foreign fighter travel is piecemeal and deeply fragmented. In other words, a foreign fighter leaving Syria might be kept out of country X but can travel freely through country Y which has not been made aware he is a suspect.

The closest the international community has come to centrally tracking foreign fighters is a through a database created last year by INTERPOL. The organization's "foreign terrorist fighter" analytic file is available on a membership basis to all 190 INTERPOL countries, each of which can add to the database and can screen against it to detect foreign fighters attempting to enter their territory.[156]

Unfortunately, only a fraction of INTERPOL countries have participated in it. Indeed, more than 25,000 foreign fighters have gone to Syria and Iraq, yet at last count INTERPOL's database only included around 5,000 names because foreign partners are reluctant to share.[157] This has to change—and quickly. Thousands of these fighters are returning home, and this database has the potential to become the global "tripwire" to detect their movements. Even the few thousand names already added to the INTERPOL database have been useful to the United States, as many of them were previously unknown to us.[158]

Recommendation: The United States must work with international partners to designate INTERPOL as a central repository for foreign fighter identities. The Administration must strongly urge partners who have shared foreign fighter data with U.S. authorities to share the same data, where possible, via INTERPOL systems with the rest of the international community. This would enhance U.S. security by ensuring more individuals of concern are stopped well before they reach American borders.

Recommendation: The Administration should conduct a classified review of the foreign fighter names known to the United States and determine whether there are any additional identities that can be added to INTERPOL's foreign fighter database. More broadly, this review should also consider whether the process in place for quickly declassifying information to place in INTERPOL systems is adequate.

Key Finding 10: *DHS is seeking to more quickly leverage the unclassified data it collects to identify high-risk individuals—including terrorists and foreign fighters—traveling to, through, and from the United States. To do so, the Department requires an interim ability to query unclassified data in classified environments.*[159]

Much of the information the U.S. government receives from foreign partners is classified, like the identities of possible terrorists. Using that information to screen for suspects must be done on secure systems. DHS has proposed an interim process which will allow intelligence analysts to tap unclassified data sets directly from classified systems and detect extremists who may have entered the country or are attempting to do so.[160] For example, a DHS analysts might want to search the manifests of planes bound for the United States for the name of a certain foreign fighter, but the analyst might not be able to do so easily if the name was received from a sensitive source overseas, making it classified. He or she would be unable to type a classified piece of data into the search box unless the system was on a classified network.[161]

The Task Force believes a temporary data transfer process should be used to address such challenges but only until the long-planned DHS data framework is capable of meeting the mission need. DHS should revert to a model with more privacy safeguards once the technical capabilities are available. We understand that access to this data in the classified domain will be limited to intelligence analysts, support staff for intelligence analysts, and CBP personnel conducting targeting and intelligence analysis. Technical personnel will be responsible for loading the data onto the classified domain and performing system administration functions, but they will not have access to the actual data after the uploading is complete.

Recommendation: DHS should expedite efforts to fully develop the DHS Data Framework so that information at all levels of classification can be used for critical counterterrorism purposes by DHS and other relevant agencies. The Department should report to Congress on its interim use of this capability, progress in developing the full framework, and any additional resources needed to complete the effort.

Key Finding 11: *The DHS Counterterrorism Advisory Board (CTAB) is the Department's key forum for fusing operations, intelligence, and policy information at a senior level to better mitigate terrorist threats; however, the CTAB's charter has not been authorized by Congress nor does it reflect recent changes to the threat environment, including the rising threat of foreign fighters and homegrown terror.*

Established in 2010, the CTAB brings together top DHS officials at the behest of the Secretary of Homeland Security to share information and coordinate counterterrorism activities. By many accounts, the CTAB has improved the Department's ability to adapt to the threat environment and keep policy responses in sync across the many DHS components. The CTAB, however, is not currently authorized in law, running the risk it could fall into disuse or stray from its core counterterrorism mandate. Moreover, its original charter does not reflect changes in the threat environment, including the surge in homegrown extremism and the threat from foreign fighters.[162] Authorization in law and updates to the charter would keep the CTAB on a strong footing so it can be best used by future DHS Secretaries and their lieutenants.

Recommendation: Congress should authorize the activities of the CTAB, and in line with the recommendations of the Homeland Security Advisory Council, ensure that its charter is reviewed and revised to reflect "(1) the current threat environment, (2) any policy changes that have been made since issuance, and (3) to align DHS CT activities under the Secretary's Unity of Effort guidance."[163]

Key Finding 12: *More can be done to incorporate valuable "financial intelligence" into counterterrorism screening and vetting processes. This data can be used to detect previously unknown extremists and to identify individuals tied to terrorism attempting to transit the United States, among other counterterrorism priorities.*

Since 9/11, significant barriers to intelligence information sharing have been reduced or eliminated across the U.S. government, allowing authorities to connect the dots to spot and interdict violent extremists seeking to do our country harm. Much of this information is leveraged during the travel screening process to screen passengers so that law enforcement can catch terrorists and foreign fighters while they are on the move. The Task Force spoke with a number of officials who have indicated that more can be done to integrate financial intelligence into the systems used to screen for terrorist travel. We support ongoing efforts to bolster this type of information sharing between federal agencies.

Recommendation: The Administration should accelerate efforts to better incorporate financial intelligence into vetting and screening systems and provide Congress with regular updates on its progress.

Key Finding 13: *State and local fusion centers are underutilized by federal law enforcement nationwide when it comes to combating the immediate foreign fighter threat and terrorist travel generally.*

In the wake of 9/11, many States and urban areas around the country established fusion centers to enhance sharing of counterterrorism information and criminal intelligence at all levels of government. The National Network of Fusion Centers now includes 78 separate centers, many of which bring together federal, state, and local law enforcement; emergency responders; public health professionals; private sector representatives; and others. Most of these centers receive federal assistance, whether through grant dollars or the support of federal intelligence analysts who sit alongside their state and local counterparts to share information.

With the terror threat becoming more diffuse nationally, fusion centers are more important than ever. Federal agencies are strained by the workload associated with monitoring the surging number of homegrown extremists, aspiring foreign fighters, returnees, and other terrorist targets. State and local partners not only can help lighten the load but are also able to provide invaluable on-the-ground assistance to mitigate terror threats.

Cooperation between fusion centers and federal law enforcement, including the FBI's Joint Terrorism Task Forces (JTTFs) has improved considerably in recent years, yet some centers still report they are underutilized and not made aware of terrorism-related investigations or activities within their respective areas of responsibility. For example, when a watchlisted individual is stopped for a traffic violation or is detected traveling through a U.S. airport, there is currently no mechanism to automatically notify the closest fusion center, even though law enforcement represented in that center may ultimately be called on to respond. The lack of automatic coordination also may deprive authorities of key local insights that could help interdict terror suspects. Similarly, fusion centers are not automatically notified when an American foreign fighter suspect returns from an overseas extremist sanctuary.

When fusion centers are used, the benefits are clear. In one recent case, federal officials received a tip that unidentified Americans from a specific state traveled overseas to fight with Islamist militants.[164] The fragmentary intelligence was passed down to the relevant fusion center. In a matter of weeks, the center pieced together information from local sources and managed to identify the suspects. They quickly notified federal counterterrorism officials, who placed the suspects on the terrorist watchlist to ensure they did not make it back into America undetected.

Recommendation: Federal law enforcement, including the FBI's JTTFs, should better leverage the National Network of Fusion Centers for assistance with terrorist-travel related matters. Stronger relationships between the two—and co-location where possible—will further enhance information-sharing and help government agencies stop extremists from entering our country and keep more Americans from leaving to join terrorist groups.

Recommendation: Federal authorities should explore providing notification to fusion centers when there are hits against the terrorist watchlist of individuals within a given fusion center's area of operations. Routine notification will give state and local partners awareness in case they are called on to assist and would create an additional opportunity for those partners to connect the dots and provide federal authorities any pertinent information they have on those subjects.

Recommendation: Federal law enforcement should regularly notify fusion centers when a "returnee" comes back to their area of operations. These individuals, who return from overseas terrorist sanctuaries, pose a potential threat to the homeland. If made aware, fusion centers can serve as a force multiplier and an additional source of information to determine whether such individuals are seeking to recruit others to join extremist groups, are planning to head back to the conflict zone, or are engaged in attack plotting.

Key Finding 14: *State and local law enforcement personnel continue to express concern that they are not provided with important counterterrorism information, whether because of a lack of security clearances, insufficient security clearance levels, or delays in security clearance processing.*

State and local law enforcement partners are essential for deterring, detecting, and disrupting terrorist travel. However, the Task Force finds there is still frustration among state and locals about the security clearance process, which is run by the federal government. Some departments with a presence at fusion centers say they have too few officers—or none—with security clearances, while others feel hamstrung by the long delays in security clearance processing.

Security clearance levels are also an issue. Most state and local law enforcement personnel who are granted security clearances are approved up to the "Secret" level. However, counterterrorism information is often classified at "Top Secret" and above, making it difficult if not impossible for those officers to assist in sensitive cases. The Task Force understands that DHS has recently decided to streamline its process and make it easier for state and local law enforcement to be granted higher clearances, where needed—a welcome development.

Recommendation: DHS, FBI, and the Director of National Intelligence's (DNI) Program Manager for the Information Sharing Environment should (1) complete a thorough review of security clearances held by non-federal Fusion Center personnel and all state and local law enforcement; and (2) provide guidance on expediting clearances to those populations and ensuring partners have the appropriate level of access.

Recommendation: DHS should regularly report to Congress on its sponsorship of Top Secret clearances for select state and local law enforcement personnel in states and major urban areas.

Prevention Activities

Actually "preventing" a known or suspected terrorist from crossing borders typically comes down to blunt law enforcement tactics: interdiction, arrest, and prosecution. If authorities lack enough evidence to detain a suspect on terror charges, they will sometimes prevent them from leaving a country by detaining them on lesser charges, such as immigration violations or making false statements to investigators.

But the foreign fighter threat has created a different dynamic. We cannot simply rely on stopping suspects when they arrive at the airport. Many of the hundreds of American who have attempted to travel to Syria and Iraq were not known to law enforcement before they traveled, and some on law enforcement's radar could not be charged without more sufficient evidence they were planning to join a foreign terrorist organization overseas.

As a result, prevention activities are increasingly important. These include efforts to help communities spot signs an individual may be seeking to join violent extremists overseas and to dissuade them from departing the country. Prevention also requires authorities to be nimble in monitoring the wide array of suspects on their radar, as a decision to join a group like ISIS is often made quickly and discretely. With extremists increasingly engaging Americans using secure communications, authorities might not be aware of a suspect's decision to travel to a terrorist hot spot, making it all-the-more important for communities to look at developing "off-ramps" to radicalization to prevent individuals from falling victim to extremist recruitment in the first place.

Key Finding 15: *The unprecedented speed at which Americans are being radicalized by violent extremists is straining federal law enforcement's ability to monitor and intercept suspects before it's too late.*

We were told repeatedly throughout our review that never before have authorities witnessed such a condensed period of radicalization, i.e., the time between an individual's first encounter with extremist propaganda to when they are prepared to act on it. Also, no official could point to another period where so many Americans have been inspired to travel overseas to become foreign fighters in a single terror hotspot.

The FBI director now says the agency is investigating ISIS supporters in all 50 states.

The scope and magnitude of terrorist recruitment worldwide is taking its toll on all law enforcement, including here in the United States. Some of our foreign partners have admitted they do not have adequate coverage on their terrorist suspects or have been forced to limit their focus to counterterrorism at the expense of investigating other criminal matters. While the circumstance are not quite as dire here, the threat environment certainly has put strain on U.S. authorities, especially at the FBI. The FBI director now says the agency is investigating ISIS supporters in all 50 states.[165]

A diffuse threat environment calls for a distributed response, which means better engaging state and local law enforcement across the country. Since 9/11, federal law enforcement has brought sheriffs' offices and police departments into the fold through improved information sharing and involvement in counterterrorism investigations. But with the continued surge in the terror threat, closer cooperation will be needed.

> **Recommendation:** Federal law enforcement agencies should rely more on state and local partners to help manage the high load of counterterrorism cases. Already police departments in major cities have reportedly begun to devote more resources to helping federal agencies keep tabs on terrorism suspects, whether to keep them from fleeing to link up with other extremists overseas or mobilizing at home. Leaders of federal departments and agencies must be clear with state and local partners about how they can best assist in this new age of terror and should also consider additional training and enhanced integration to better leverage law enforcement partners around the country.

Key Finding 16: *The majority of recent disruptions of aspiring U.S. foreign fighters occurred because of—or were aided by—warnings to law enforcement, whether from family, friends, informants, or the general public. Nevertheless, few initiatives exist nationwide to raise community awareness in order to keep more individuals from being recruited to join overseas terrorist organizations.*

A lot of cases we've disrupted, it's because somebody tipped us off.

SENIOR ADMINISTRATION OFFICAL TOLD TASK FORCE

Information from the public is crucial for stopping foreign fighter flows. "A lot of cases we've disrupted, it's because somebody tipped us off," explained one senior Administration official who spoke with the Task Force.[166] The FBI, DHS, and other agencies have done commendable investigative work to identify extremists, but without community engagement their work is considerably more difficult.

Unfortunately, the Administration relies on small initiatives with few staff, shoestring budgets, and limited records of success to spread awareness about the threat. The "Community Awareness Brief" is the federal government's primary domestic outreach effort to address domestic radicalization and inform communities about terrorist recruiting. Officials have compared it to a "D.A.R.E. program" for counterterrorism, but it has only been presented in a small number of cities.[167] Usually delivered by a handful of DHS and NCTC staffers, the brief is sometimes followed by a Community Resilience Exercise designed to engage participants in mock scenarios involving the radicalization of a community member. Unfortunately, resource constraints have kept these initiatives from being scaled beyond one-off presentations held intermittently around the country.

Moreover, departments and agencies have not done enough to successfully enlist nongovernmental partners in prevention efforts. Several NGOs, including the Countering Extremism Project and the World Organization for Resource Development and Education (WORDE), are involved in this space, but the Administration has done little to help them mature or accelerate their efforts. Major foundations, which could bring resources to bear on the problem, have also rarely been contacted by U.S. authorities on the subject.

> **Recommendation:** DHS should use the National Network of Fusion Centers to more widely deploy initiatives such as the U.S. government's Community Awareness Brief and Community Resilience Exercise, designed to increase local understanding of the foreign fighter threat. Training fusion center staff around the country to help conduct these briefings could help to increase community awareness and buy-in from local community participants.

> **Recommendation:** DHS, in consultation with other departments and agencies, should devise new approaches for encouraging community members to report suspicious activity, especially signs an individual is preparing to travel overseas to join a foreign terrorist organization. In considering new methods for engagement, authorities should also rely on lessons from the Department of Justice's (DOJ) Building Communities of Trust initiative, recognizing that one of the major barriers to cooperation in some communities is distrust of law enforcement.

Key Finding 17: *The federal government has failed to develop clear intervention strategies such as "off-ramps" to radicalization as an alternative to detaining individuals seeking to travel to fight with extremists overseas.*

Countries around the world have developed programs to address radicalization by intervening before a suspect becomes violent or enlists with a terrorist group. In some cases, these programs are also aimed at rehabilitating foreign fighters who have returned from overseas. Some of these efforts are a step too far for the United States. For Constitutional and policy reasons, the U.S. government should be wary about running its own "de-radicalization" programs for individuals who, in some cases, may simply be engaging in speech and actions protected by the First Amendment. Family, friends, and community members are often far better suited than government officials to intervene and prevent individuals from radicalizing to violence.

But U.S. authorities are still faced with the reality that every day they are investigating suspects who have been radicalized by terrorist groups and could suddenly seek to become fighters on foreign battlefields or commit acts of terror here at home. The traditional wait-and-see approach is a blunt and risky one: suspects are either arrested and prosecuted—or they are not. In only a handful of recent cases have federal authorities sought to intervene earlier to engage family or community members in dissuading a suspect from heading overseas to join ISIS or al Qaeda.

We believe more should be done to develop "off-ramps" to radicalization, particularly as terrorist groups are increasingly recruiting young people under the age of 18.

We believe more should be done to develop "off-ramps" to radicalization, particularly as terrorist groups are increasingly recruiting people under the age of 18. While recognizing that we cannot just look the other way, our only choice should not be to incarcerate teenagers on terror charges when they are preyed upon by online jihadists. Investigators, prosecutors, and judges need additional options so they can tailor their actions to the specifics of each case.

Authorities have made some attempts to pursue alternatives to prosecution, but they do not appear to be based on any overarching guidance or best-practices. In a handful of cases for instance, federal authorities have engaged with parents when it appears their children might be Syria-bound. In a case this year, an 18-year old Minnesota resident accused of attempting to join ISIS was released to a halfway house while awaiting trial, instead of being held in jail. There he received counseling and courses in civic education—but from an organization with no prior experience dealing with would-be foreign fighters.[168] The experiment fell apart when he was found with a knife hidden in his room. The accused is now back in jail, though still participating in civics lessons.[169]

So far, these efforts to pursue "off-ramps" have been ad hoc and lack a systematic framework. This is a problem. We cannot have law enforcement and justice officials developing intervention strategies on-the-fly out in the field, especially when they are swamped with counterterrorism cases and ill-equipped to develop such strategies. Instead, policymakers in Washington should take the lead in developing baseline policy and legal guidance for appropriate interventions. This includes engaging with NGOs, civil rights groups, and civil liberties advocates to ensure intervention guidance is appropriate and methods are effective.

The FBI recently announced plans to refer more suspects—particularly juveniles—to interventions by involving community leaders, educators, mental health professionals, religious leaders, parents, and peers, depending on the circumstances.[170] In these cases, the FBI will not necessarily cease its criminal investigation and will remain alert to suspects who might become dangerous or plan to travel to join extremists overseas.[171] We are glad the FBI is taking additional steps to engage communities on interventions, but the framework for implementing these efforts remains unclear.

> **Recommendation:** The Administration should take immediate steps to develop a baseline policy and legal framework for intervening in cases of potential violent radicalization, rather than relying on ad hoc interventions. This guidance should be produced by DHS, FBI, DOJ, and the NCTC—in consultation with other departments and agencies and nongovernmental organizations—distributed to appropriate parties, and incorporated into field training where applicable. This guidance must clearly spell out the legal parameters for interveners, particularly as they could expose themselves to liability if interventions fail.[172] Moreover, from this framework, the U.S. government should develop a "playbook" regarding violent extremist cases outlining the array of options available to families, communities, law enforcement, prosecutors, and judges to dissuade, deter, or disrupt an individual at different stages along the path to violent extremism.

Key Finding 18: *Aspiring foreign fighters are increasingly being radicalized and recruited by extremists overseas via websites and apps with secure private messaging features. The result is that law enforcement faces greater difficulty accessing extremist communications, making it harder to disrupt violent plots and terrorist travel.*

The world is witnessing sweeping changes in extremist tactics, not least of which is the concept of crowd-sourced recruiting. As detailed in the "Threat" section of this report, terrorist groups like ISIS seek to identify possible recruits by issuing a call to arms to their thousands of social media followers, including on Twitter, Facebook, YouTube, and beyond. Then they engage promising radicals via direct message, communicating with them privately to determine their willingness to engage in jihad or persuade them to travel overseas. Finally, terrorist recruiters direct their subjects to use encrypted apps and hidden websites to prevent monitoring of their further conversations and plotting.

This last stage is especially concerning. Extremists are using freely available communications tools to hide illegal activities, such as funneling young operatives to and from terrorist safe havens or planning to kill Americans within the homeland. Even faced with lawful warrants from the courts to access those communications, some companies are unable to comply because of built-in security and encryption. In some cases, technology is creating a virtual safe haven for terrorists to communicate around the world. The FBI has been especially vocal in highlighting these challenges as the terror threat level has risen.[173]

The "going dark" problem has stirred an important debate in this country about how technological changes are affecting privacy and public safety. We are not satisfied these challenges have been discussed as thoroughly and openly as they should be. Law enforcement and technology companies seem to be talking past each other, and no sustained dialogue has been established on the subject between key parties, including Congress, law enforcement, and private industry. American people deserve to see their leaders tackle this subject openly and through a robust dialogue.

> **Recommendation:** A sustained and open dialogue and enhanced cooperation is needed between all relevant parties—including Congress, law enforcement, and private industry—to discuss challenges and find concrete solutions to the "going dark" problem, with the ultimate goals of maintaining cybersecurity, protecting civil liberties, and ensuring public safety, especially against terrorist threats to the United States.

Key Finding 19: *The Administration has launched public counter-messaging efforts at the State Department to push back against terrorist propaganda overseas, yet more needs to be done domestically.*

> It used to be the assessment of the [intelligence community] that you could not go all the way down the path to radicalization without personal contact. But that's all changed.
>
> SENIOR ADMINISTRATION OFFICAL TOLD TASK FORCE

Terrorist organizations are recruiting online and across borders at a level we have never seen before. Thousands of citizens from more than 100 countries have already been drawn to fight with extremists in Syria and Iraq without ever meeting an ISIS "recruiter" face-to-face. U.S. officials who spoke with our Task Force say many if not most of the Americans who have been inspired to join groups like ISIS were radicalized online, not from someone in their communities, and the case studies we reviewed seem to support that claim.[174] "It used to be the assessment of the [intelligence community] that you could not go all the way down the path to radicalization without personal contact," one official told us. "But that's all changed."[175] In an age of peer-to-peer radicalization, the new battlespace is online, and the United States must work openly and aggressively to contest it.

Overseas, the State Department has launched a counter-messaging campaign to challenge terrorist recruitment and propaganda, especially on social media. The Center for Strategic Counterterrorism Communications (CSCC) leads the effort and says it primarily targets individuals who are "on the fence" about traveling to enlist with extremist groups by using hard facts to expose their deception and the danger of enlisting in their ranks. The CSCC has started to engage foreign partners to counter extremist misinformation using more organic and credible approaches. Furthermore, the United States can learn from foreign partner governments which have engaged in their own counter-messaging efforts.

But the CSCC has a staff of only a few dozen, compared to the tens of thousands of online ISIS followers who amplify the terrorist group's content. Its efforts have also been pilloried for being slow, bureaucratic, and ineffective at combating the viral success of ISIS propaganda.[176] What is more worrisome is that State Department officials told the Task Force that under existing authorities they do not believe they can use the Center's resources to directly engage with Americans online.[177] In other words, the State Department can discourage foreigners from joining ISIS but not dissuade U.S. citizens.

We do not believe counter-messaging is solely or even primarily the job of the U.S. government. In fact, tweets and YouTube videos with the seal of the United States will likely be discredited by budding extremists. However, the federal government can help set the tone, share best practices from foreign partners, and most importantly jump-start efforts by non-governmental organizations (NGOs) and other private sector partners to push back against terrorist recruitment and propaganda within our borders.

> **Recommendation:** The Administration should ramp up counter-messaging efforts here at home and urgently develop ways to empower nongovernmental organizations to contest the propaganda of violent groups seeking to radicalize and recruit Americans to travel to overseas terrorist safe havens. As part of this effort, the Administration should also seek to work with non-traditional partners, including universities, the private sector, and philanthropic foundations.
>
> **Recommendation:** The Administration should work more closely with social media companies—including

those who are not routinely engaged by government agencies but whose platforms are often used by extremists[178]—and urge them to accelerate the removal of violent-extremist content which violates their terms of service, whether through tools which make it easier for users to flag inappropriate material or by devoting greater internal resources to identifying and removing offending content and users.

Key Finding 20: *Unlike many countries, the U.S. government has made little use of disaffected extremists to dissuade others from traveling to fight in terrorist sanctuaries.*

The Task Force found a number of our foreign partners have engaged "jaded jihadists" and returnees from the battlefield to tell their stories and convince others not to travel to terrorist safe havens. These individuals are likely viewed by potential extremists as more credible voices than governments. Therefore, they stand a better chance of dissuading likely or future jihadists from coming under the influence of groups like ISIS.

We were disappointed however to find key U.S. departments and agencies have done little to leverage the stories of American returnees or family members of those who have fled to the conflict zone. In fact, one counterterrorism official even admitted to the Task Force that counter-messaging teams had not reached out to DOJ or FBI to see if any disaffected extremists on their radar would tell their stories publicly.[179] Only very recently does that appear to have changed, though we are unaware of any meaningful progress.

Fortunately, the State Department has begun to shift its content in this direction, launching a series of ISIS defector YouTube videos.[180] The videos include footage from interviews and news stories featuring individuals who were horrified to witness ISIS oppression up close. But these testimonials have received relatively little attention when posted from State Department social media accounts. One such video only received 500 views despite being posted for two months; by comparison, a recent ISIS execution video received tens of thousands of views within hours of going online.

Grassroots messaging has a better chance than government missives of reaching vulnerable young people, as noted earlier. Accordingly, U.S. authorities must empower nongovernmental and non-traditional partners to do this kind of outreach. For instance, a UK-based foundation recently sponsored an ISIS counter-messaging campaign—#NotAnotherBrother—which showcases the "reality of life as a foreign fighter."[181] The slick, privately produced video has drawn far more attention worldwide when compared with similar U.S.-government-produced content.

> **Recommendation:** The Administration should launch a concerted effort to use the testimonials of disaffected "former" foreign fighters, extremists, and their friends and relatives to counter the narratives that persuade Americans to travel overseas to fight with extremist groups. Most importantly, the Administration should help facilitate and distribute these stories through nongovernmental channels where possible and empower non-traditional partners to do the same. Departments and agencies should also work with foreign partners to get permission to use narratives which they have produced featuring their own citizens.

Key Finding 21: *Many Western countries have begun to use passport revocation as a means to keep aspiring foreign fighters from traveling, but the tool has been little-used by U.S. authorities.*

A number of Western governments have taken direct action to stop suspects by taking away their means of travel: passports. Australia, Britain, Canada, France, Germany, and others have used this tool as a last resort when they think extremists might take off for the conflict zone but when there is limited ability to prosecute them in advance. For example, Australian authorities confiscated the passport of a Musa Cerantonio, a vocal ISIS recruiter and jihadist preacher, after he reportedly tried to flee to Syria in June 2014; he made it to the Philippines before being deported back to Australia.[182]

The U.S. government has the ability under the law to revoke passports on a number of different grounds, including for national security purposes.[183] But unlike some foreign partners, American authorities cannot make this decision unilaterally. The Supreme Court has ruled that an individual's right to travel cannot be violated without due process, which has been interpreted to mean an American passport cannot be revoked without giving the suspect a chance to contest the evidence against him or her.[184] There appear to be few public cases of passports being revoked on national security grounds, which could be explained by the fact that national security and counterterrorism investigations often involve classified information. Law enforcement agencies face difficult trade-offs when deciding whether to use classified information in court, as noted elsewhere in this report.

This does not mean the tool has never been used. The U.S. State Department revoked the passport of Anwar al-Awlaki, a top al Qaeda in the Arabian Peninsula leader, nearly six months before he was killed in a drone strike in Yemen. First though, the Department sent a cable to its embassy in Yemen directing that it send a message "to Mr. [Awlaki] informing him that there is an important letter for him at post regarding his U.S. passport."[185] Presumably if Awlaki had shown up, he would have been served with a passport revocation letter and later been given the opportunity to contest the charges against him. He never showed, and the passport was revoked.

Passport revocation is not the only way to make it difficult for a suspect to travel. America's advanced watchlisting system, discussed earlier, allows authorities to flag foreign-fighter suspects in a secure database and to be notified when any of them attempt to fly out of the country on their passports. Moreover, with enough evidence, a watchlisted terror suspect can be upgraded to the no-fly list, which automatically prevents them from boarding an aircraft.

But if an American has already left the United States for Syria, adding their name to the watchlist may not do much good in keeping them from getting the rest way to the battlefield. The majority of Americans who have attempted to fight in Syria and Iraq managed to leave the country before being stopped by U.S. law enforcement; only later did many of them come to the attention of authorities. Many are presumably still able to travel on their passports if the documents have not been cancelled, making it easier for them to return to the West. On the other hand, when an individual's passport is revoked, a government can alert nearly all other countries via INTERPOL that the document is no longer valid and should not be accepted, theoretically constraining a suspect's international mobility.

The Task Force is concerned about the gap between passport revocation and watchlisting. The latter is not an equal substitute for the former. We must assume suspects dead set on joining a terrorist group in Syria and Iraq could eventually find a way out of the United States. In those cases, we need to be able to make it more difficult for them to travel the remainder of the way to the conflict zone and, ultimately, prevent them from returning to the West undetected.

> **Recommendation:** The Administration should conduct a review of its passport revocation policies and procedures which could be used in cases involving terrorist travel and foreign fighters and report to Congress on any changes desired to streamline and improve the process while protecting due process rights and civil liberties. This review should consider similar actions undertaken by foreign partners and also propose alternatives to passport revocation which could have a similar effect in slowing or obstructing terrorist travel across borders.

DETECTION & DISRUPTION

If terrorists and foreign fighters cannot be deterred from crossing borders, then the United States must be able to detect and disrupt them when they do. This requires real-time counterterrorism information to be used at border checkpoints, airports, and beyond to spot travelers who have been flagged. It also requires shrewd analysis of travel patterns and the identification of suspicious behavior. This is no easy task. More than half a billion people cross borders into the United States each year, 330 million of which are non-citizens.[186] Catching the small number who have ties to terrorism requires close cooperation at all levels of government.

America failed to adequately integrate counterterrorism information at the borders before 9/11, a vulnerability which allowed extremists to travel back-and-forth to the United States undetected by law enforcement. In fact, the 9/11 Commission concluded 15 of the 19 hijackers were "potentially vulnerable to interception by border authorities" but were not detected because of "systemic weaknesses" in the U.S. border system.[187] But extraordinary progress has been made since then. Law enforcement agencies now conduct national security checks on virtually every traveler—whether they are a foreign national applying for a visa or an American returning home—before they board flights to ensure they do not have ties to terrorism. Moreover, U.S. border officers are deployed to a number of countries overseas to detect threats early by pushing the screening process outward.

The danger from foreign fighters requires us to reexamine these systems to keep suspects from slipping through the cracks. The Task Force found several potential weaknesses in U.S. detection and disruption efforts. For instance, more could be done to tackle the challenge of "broken travel," where extremists switch planes and destinations to avoid law enforcement detection, and authorities could put in place measures to weed out violent extremists earlier in the visa application process.

Pre-Travel Phase

Pre-travel screening allows authorities to conduct advance security checks to identify high-risk individuals who might be connected to violent extremist groups. In some ways, pre-travel security screening is more important than the physical screening of a traveler. Most terrorist suspects and foreign fighters are not carrying weapons or explosive when they fly. Authorities are more likely to detect them by searching counterterrorism databases than by searching duffel bags for illicit materials. We believe additional enhancements can be made to detect threats in the pre-travel phase and to prevent extremists from taking advantage of legal travel routes into our country.

Key Finding 22: *Substantial progress has been made since 9/11 to enhance visa security and conduct advance counterterrorism reviews of foreign nationals seeking to visit the United States. The Task Force believes there may be additional opportunities to expand screening to identify potential extremists earlier in the process.*

To visit the United States, citizens of most countries must obtain visas, which are issued at overseas embassies and consulates by the State Department. In 2014, the State Department granted nearly 10 million visas to foreigners seeking temporary entry into America (and nearly 500,000 immigrant visas for permanent residence).[188] This involves submitting an online questionnaire, scheduling an interview at a U.S. embassy or consulate, providing biographic and biometric information (such as fingerprints), and awaiting a formal decision. The process can take anywhere from a few days to a few weeks.[189]

The visa issuance process represents a critical stage for law enforcement to detect individuals with terrorist ties and prevent them from entering the United States. Many of the subjects who have been convicted on terrorism charges in the United States since 9/11 are foreign-born individuals who traveled to America on visas—whether on student visas, tourist visas, or for legal permanent residence. Some had potentially detectable terrorist connections beforehand, and others committed visa fraud by providing false information.

All visa applications are screened extensively against criminal and counterterrorism databases, though this was not always the case. For a number of years before and after 9/11, the State Department only screened an applicant's basic information and to see if he or she matched a name on a terrorist watchlist; as a result, approximately two percent of visa applications were flagged to receive a more extensive counterterrorism review.[190] If a visa was approved, it was not typically screened against classified databases again. Today the State Department forwards 100 percent of visa applications to NCTC for deeper, more sophisticated screening to uncover possible terrorism connections.[191] The Department also continuously checks visas against government databases in case new information is discovered tying an individual to terrorist activity. These improvements have led to the denial of thousands of U.S. visas due to counterterrorism concerns, some of which may not otherwise have been detected.[193]

In higher-risk foreign countries, the U.S. government has implemented an added defensive measure, the Visa Security Program (VSP). VSP is run by DHS in 19 countries and aims to do more in-depth counterterrorism screening to keep violent extremists from gaining entry into America. At these higher-threat locations, visa applications undergo a more rigorous screening process, including an immediate national security review when their immigration application is submitted online, which allows Immigration and Customs Enforcement (ICE) agents to flag concerns with an applicant even before they show up at the embassy for an interview. The additional time and manpower of Visa Security Units (VSUs) allows for suspicious applicants to be vetted more thoroughly. Once DHS has made a determination on the applicant, it provides the State Department with a recommendation on the individual's admissibility.[194]

VSP runs applications through a system called PATRIOT (Pre-Adjudicated Threat Recognition and Intelligence Operations Team) well before State Department officers review the applications. PATRIOT culls through public safety, criminal, and national security databases and gives analysts in Washington, D.C. the opportunity to do a deeper review to ensure U.S. authorities do not have information on an applicant that would be reason to deny them entry into the country. When an application is flagged through the VSP, an officer at the relevant U.S. overseas post is assigned to it and can do additional work on-the-ground in the host country to resolve any concerns.[195]

The Task Force believes the VSP is a valuable additional layer of security. We also recognize the VSP could be expensive to deploy globally, given that DHS prefers to have an agent on the ground to conduct follow-on reviews after an application is initially screened. However, we believe the up-front screening that occurs as part of the VSP—an immediate and automatic national security review of each visa application through the PATRIOT system—does not need to be limited to only the 19 existing VSP countries when there are 225 U.S. visa-issuing posts worldwide.

Over time, PATRIOT screening could be expanded virtually to all visa-issuing posts worldwide and provide an extra layer of security to help State Department officers decide which individuals should be granted entry into the United States and which should not. Under the current system, a full counterterrorism review sometimes does not occur until weeks after an application is submitted; near-instant security checks would help give the U.S. government additional lead time to do background investigation on applications which get flagged, offering more opportunities to uncover previously unknown terrorist ties. The VSP program has already helped identify new terrorist tactics and has provided additional information on known extremists, so we believe finding a way to deploy some elements globally would yield additional national security benefits.

> **Recommendation:** DHS, in conjunction with the Department of State, should strengthen security screening of travelers who require a visa by working to deploy virtual elements of the VSP globally, specifically through the expanded use of the PATRIOT screening system. PATRIOT is currently used for remote screening; however it only supports locations in which VSP units currently exist. DHS should consider expanding the use of the system to additional high-risk embassies and consulates where VSP units may not currently have a presence.[196] DHS should also explore conducting full VSP reviews using more cost-effective means— particularly by training other U.S. government personnel to do the on-the-ground VSP assessments in countries where DHS has a more limited presence.

Key Finding 23: *The Administration has improved the security of the Visa Waiver Program (VWP), but continuous enhancements must be made to keep pace with changing terrorist tactics and to detect violent extremists before they board U.S.-bound planes.*

Some critics have labeled the VWP the "Achilles' heel" of U.S. security out of fear that foreign fighters from those countries will be able to slip into the United States undetected. It is true that most European jihadists who have fought in Syria are from VWP countries, and although such residents can get into America with greater ease, they are still subjected to security checks. Moreover, their home countries must implement travel security enhancements in order to participate in the program.

Citizens of VWP countries can travel to the United States for up to 90 days without having to obtain an entry visa; in return, U.S. citizens must also be allowed to travel visa-free to the participating country. VWP countries tend to be developed economies that are viewed as a low security threat to America, and the program brings substantial economic benefits to the United States and participating nations.

In place of a visa, VWP travelers must fill out the Electronic System for Travel Authorization (ESTA), when booking travel to the United States. This online form provides key information on each traveler to U.S. authorities and is screened against terrorist watchlists and criminal databases. Due to the heightened concerns about foreign fighters, DHS announced in November 2014 that VWP travelers would be required to submit additional information, including aliases, citizenships, parents' names, national identification number, contact information, employment information, and city of birth.[197] Additional information makes it easier for law enforcement to identify terrorists and to expedite legitimate travel. Moreover, ESTA forms are continuously screened against the watchlist and other security databases to ensure no new ties to terrorism are detected after an individual has been approved.[198]

There are currently *38 VWP countries, 30 of which are in Europe.*[199] To participate, the U.S. government requires that countries meet several standards and implement security improvements, including: (1) issuing their residents secure, machine-readable passports; (2) having less than a three percent visa-refusal rate into the United States; (3) reporting lost/stolen passports; (4) sharing information with U.S. authorities on travelers (including criminals and known or suspected terrorists); (5) requiring its residents to fill out an online authorization form, ESTA, before traveling to the United States; and (6) increasing their own airport security requirements.

VISA WAIVER PROGRAM (VWP) COUNTRIES

Andorra	Estonia	Italy	Netherlands	South Korea
Australia	Finland	Japan	New Zealand	Spain
Austria	France	Latvia	Norway	Sweden
Belgium	Germany	Liechtenstein	Portugal	Switzerland
Brunei	Greece	Lithuania	San Marino	Taiwan
Chile	Hungary	Luxembourg	Singapore	United Kingdom
Czech Republic	Iceland	Malta	Slovakia	
Denmark	Ireland	Monaco	Slovenia	

Many officials believe the VWP actually *enhances* rather than weakens U.S. security against terrorist travel. In particular, all participating countries are required to regularly share information that they might not normally provide, including: intelligence about terrorists; biographic, biometric, and criminal data; and information on lost and stolen passports. This data helps to prevent violent extremists from entering the United States. DHS also recently announced VWP countries would soon be required to begin issuing their citizens fraud-resistant e-passports, to regularly screen against INTERPOL's Stolen and Lost Travel Document Database, and to permit additional federal air marshals on flights from their countries to the United States.[200]

We believe DHS and the Administration have been attentive to the need for security improvements to the VWP. But given that the threat environment has changed and continues to evolve, we strongly urge the Department to remain vigilant and to consider additional security measures.

Recommendation: The Administration should continuously explore further changes to the process for screening visa-free travelers, including additional security improvements to ESTA. Elsewhere in this report, the Task Force makes additional recommendations which might improve the overall security of the VWP and leverage it to obstruct terrorist and foreign fighter travel overseas, including those detailed under Key Findings 8, 29, 30, and 31.

Recommendation: The Secretary of Homeland Security, in consultation with the Secretary of State, should enforce VWP eligibility reviews for certain countries annually rather than every two years and should provide annual intelligence and threat assessments, in consultation with the DNI, of high-risk VWP countries. These assessments should include travel vulnerabilities which may be exploited by terrorists, as well as each country's overall compliance with VWP obligations. The foreign fighter threat has shown how quickly a country deemed "low-risk" for terrorist travel can quickly become a "high-risk" source country for violent extremists.

Recommendation: DHS should work with Congress to give the Secretary explicit authority to temporarily suspend a country's VWP status for failure to share counterterrorism information. As it currently stands, the Secretary is not granted explicit authority in the law to suspend a country's status for failing to pass along information that is critical for stopping terrorist movements, even though countries have agreed to provide such information as a condition of participation in the program. If the Secretary had clearer suspension authority it would be a more credible tool to encourage partners to comply with security requirements. The Secretary should also continue to use the current foreign fighter threat as an opportunity to regularly remind participating VWP countries of their obligations under the program.

Recommendation: DHS should explore strengthening the security of the ESTA application by introducing mechanisms to instantly verify the data provided by applicants. Such tools are already standard on many internet-based forms and sign-ups. Data validation, for instance, could easily be introduced to confirm an applicant's email address or mobile phone number through a confirmation code to be re-entered on the form. This would give authorities greater confidence in the information supplied by applicants, particularly individuals who might be supplying false information. DHS should also engage with private sector companies who provide online tools capable of "deception detection" on web-based forms.

Key Finding 24: *U.S. law enforcement and intelligence agencies remain concerned about terrorists posing as refugees. Agencies have made improvements to the refugee security screening process, but more must be done to mitigate potential vulnerabilities.*

Members of terrorist groups like ISIS have publicly bragged they are working to sneak operatives into the West posing as refugees, and European officials are worried this is already the case.

Members of terrorist groups like ISIS have publicly bragged they are working to sneak operatives into the West posing as refugees, and European officials are worried this is already the case.[201] The Task Force recognizes terrorist infiltration into the United States through the refugee process is less likely than other routes and more time intensive for extremists, but these threats must be kept in mind during the refugee screening process. Such tactics would not be new for terrorist groups, and more than four million people have fled the conflict zone in Syria, offering extremists ample opportunity to blend into migrant groups.

America has a proud tradition of welcoming refugees, especially those fleeing war and violence in their home countries. However we also must remain vigilant that we do not inadvertently grant admission into our country to violent extremists seeking to do our people harm. Fighters belonging to ISIS's predecessor, al Qaeda in Iraq, successfully slipped into the United States through the refugee resettlement program in 2009, when two terrorist responsible for killing U.S. troops in Iraq were granted entry and settled in Kentucky. Only later did the FBI and DHS discover this error and arrest the suspects after finding their fingerprints matched those found on IEDs in Iraq.[202]

Law enforcement and intelligence officials have expressed concern publicly and privately to Task Force Members that our refugee screening process has inherent vulnerabilities, particularly in war-torn countries where we have little intelligence on the ground. The lack of information makes it difficult to conduct high-confidence background checks on potential refugees.[203] In other words, we cannot screen against information we do not have. In these cases, departments and agencies should establish clear plans to enhance background reviews and outline how domestic agencies like the FBI will be involved in mitigating any risks associated with populations of concern which are granted entry.

> **Recommendation:** The Administration should provide a report to Congress highlighting the refugee routes most vulnerable to terrorist exploitation based on intelligence, detailing the state of the refugee vetting process for those countries, and outlining plans to mitigate any vulnerabilities in the system.

Travel Phase

America has sought to build out a "layered" defense against terrorist travel and has made considerable improvements since the early 2000s. Indeed, passengers traveling to, from, and within the United States are subject to security screening procedures—some seen and some unseen—at virtually every stage in their journey. These measures include watchlist vetting, automated targeting to identify high-risk passengers, physical traveler and baggage screening, federal air marshal protection, and other security layers.

In the wake of past security breaches, passengers are now vetted against counterterrorism databases at multiple stages throughout their journey, potentially including after they have booked their ticket, when they check in at the airport, once the aircraft departs, and—for those headed into the country—at the border and immigration checkpoint. Continuous checks allow law enforcement to spot suspicious travel patterns and ensure real-time intelligence can be fused into the process to stop terrorist suspects who are on the move.[204]

Despite improvements, the foreign fighter threat has stressed the system. Terrorists are changing their tactics, and authorities are having a harder time tracking them. The Task Force commends DHS in particular for stepping up efforts to interdict terrorists and foreign fighters, but we believe additional steps can be taken to tighten security in the travel phase.

Key Finding 25: *Aspiring foreign fighters are increasingly using "broken travel" and other evasive tactics, making it difficult for authorities to detect and disrupt their movements.*

Earlier this year, INTERPOL chief Juergen Stock warned the UN Security Council about "broken travel," explaining that foreign fighters were increasingly using circuitous routes and middlemen to get to and from the conflict zone.[205] For example, an aspiring American foreign fighter might book a roundtrip ticket from New York to Athens, but skip the return flight and instead drive through Turkey to get to Syria. This can make it harder for law enforcement to track suspects. "It is a concern," explained DHS intelligence chief Frank Taylor at a Committee hearing this year. "People can book a flight to an end-destination...and go other places."[206] U.S. officials testifying before the Committee in February also emphasized extremists are varying their routes using combinations of air, land, and sea transportation.[207]

We are concerned the international travel system is not well-suited for detecting broken travel and similar approaches used by terrorists and foreign fighters. Spotting such tactics requires close and continuous information sharing between countries regarding passenger manifests, screening data, and other information that some do not even routinely collect. The problem does not appear to have an easy solution, but closer multilateral information exchanges—at least in cases of known or suspected terrorists—might help illuminate terror travel routes and result in better tracking of suspects.

> **Recommendation:** U.S. authorities must engage with air carriers and foreign partners to discuss enhancing air passenger targeting systems, information sharing, and additional protocols that might make it easier to spot extremists' broken travel tactics. Federal law enforcement and intelligence agencies should undertake a concerted effort to ensure all relevant travel data is being leveraged to uncover extremists' evasive transit patterns. Other governments, especially in Europe, can address this challenge by improving collection of passenger data, as discussed in the "Overseas Gaps" section of this report, and sharing it in counterterrorism cases.

Key Finding 26: *More could be done to give frontline operators better intelligence reach-back capabilities so DHS can "connect the dots" and uncover previously unidentified terrorists and foreign fighters using information obtained at border checkpoints.*

DHS Customs and Border Protection (CBP) officers currently have the ability to pass along suspicious information collected at the borders for analysts to review. However, the process is not fully automated, and it does not take full advantage of the government's array of criminal-intelligence and travel databases, meaning that important connections could be getting missed.

For example, an officer might interview a suspicious passenger in secondary screening and receive a phone number for the place the passenger is staying while in the country. While the traveler himself might not pop up on a terrorist watchlist, the phone number might be connected to a known terrorist facilitator. But even if the CBP officer passed along his interview data to analysts, existing systems might not be able to make the terrorism connection. Indeed, CBP still does not have full, automated access to some sensitive databases or to certain useful collections of travel data held by other departments and agencies.

The above scenario is a hypothetical. Nevertheless we believe it is important for CBP officers to have the ability to easily and quickly transmit information gained during inspections to be fully vetted for national security reasons. This means the agency must have access—or reach-back—to all relevant unclassified and classified systems needed to uncover previously unknown terrorism connections, especially when engaging with high-risk subjects.

> **Recommendation:** DHS should work with other relevant agencies to provide Congress with a plan to better integrate intelligence and law enforcement information into CBP's counterterrorism screening processes. This plan should improve CBP's ability to fully vet discrete pieces of information acquired during inspections. The Department should also consider co-locating of some of its vetting personnel with other agencies to facilitate closer collaboration and information sharing.

Key Finding 27: *U.S. authorities continue to "push the border outward" by deploying homeland security initiatives overseas, like CBP's Preclearance program. Expanding such initiatives could help detect threats sooner.*

The Task Force commends DHS for working to increase the use of the Preclearance program at overseas airports with flights to the United States. In the select locations where it has been established, the Preclearance program allows overseas-based CBP officers to screen all passengers and luggage before a flight takes off for the United States. Officers are able to use the same authorities they would have if the inspections were conducted on U.S. soil.

CBP currently has 15 Preclearance locations in six countries, including Ireland, Aruba, The Bahamas, Bermuda, Canada, and the United Arab Emirates. However the foreign fighter threat has shown many other locations to be far more vulnerable to terrorist travel than those currently covered by the program. We are pleased that DHS announced plans earlier this year to seek an expansion of preclearance operations to 10 new airports, including to high-risk terror transit countries like Turkey.²⁰⁶ The Department should keep Congress apprised of these negotiations and continue to refine its risk-based methodology for choosing new sites.

> **Recommendation:** DHS should continue with its efforts to expand preclearance operations, should maintain rigorous risk-based selection criteria, and should provide Congress with a clear and continuing justification for selecting additional locations.

Key Finding 28: *Federal authorities use the International Criminal Police Organization's (INTERPOL) databases frequently for counterterrorism purposes, but only a fraction of U.S. states have access to INTERPOL's systems. Expansion to more states could help detect wanted foreign fighters who have slipped past border security.*

INTERPOL oversees systems—including terrorist and criminal databases and a worldwide database of lost and stolen passports—that are crucial global tools for combating terrorist and foreign fighter travel (for more detail, see Key Finding 31). Currently, all travelers entering and exiting the United States are screened against these systems. Federal law enforcement agencies also have worked in recent years to extend INTERPOL screening beyond the border by giving other government partners access to the system.

However, we found that fewer than a quarter of U.S. states currently have access to INTERPOL systems. Those which do can use the databases to catch wanted international fugitives during law enforcement stops or to ensure individuals are not presenting fraudulent travel documents to get drivers licenses. These tools could help more state and local agencies identify violent extremist who may have entered the country undetected or under a different alias.

> **Recommendation:** The Administration should report to Congress in its next budget request how it will empower INTERPOL Washington to work with a broader slate of state and local partners to expand access to INTERPOL's systems, especially for counterterrorism purposes.

> **Recommendation:** The Administration should consider granting State and local law enforcement the ability to quickly submit INTERPOL notices for wanted subjects in their jurisdictions. Aspiring foreign fighters often leave for the conflict zone with little or no notice, and giving state and local partners the ability to expedite notices to INTERPOL's 190 member states could help stop extremists in their tracks on the way to terrorist safe havens, especially in cases where local authorities are tipped off to a suspect who was not previously on federal law enforcement's radar.

OVERSEAS GAPS

The Task Force's biggest concern is that foreign governments have not done enough to close conspicuous security gaps which are susceptible to extremist exploitation. These weaknesses make it easier for Americans to get to jihadist battlefields and increase the threat of extremists traveling undetected and reaching U.S. soil. Many of our foreign partners remain in a "pre-9/11" counterterrorism posture, with security gaps that mirror our own from 15 years ago. Barriers between intelligence and police prevent information sharing in some countries, while in others lax counterterrorism screening at airports and border crossings makes it easier for extremists to slip through undetected. Additionally, some countries still do not even criminalize participation in international terrorism, making it difficult to jail foreign fighters.

Over the past decade, the U.S. government has provided billions of dollars in counterterrorism assistance to foreign partners, especially to disrupt terrorist travel. For example, the State Department and DHS have helped other governments screen passengers against terrorist watchlists and strengthen border security. Similarly, DOJ has deployed its legal experts worldwide to advise foreign officials on crafting and enforcing counterterrorism laws. In many places these efforts have been successful, but the Task Force is concerned assistance efforts have been uncoordinated and lack overarching strategic guidance.

Recognizing overseas gaps, the Obama Administration pushed the UN Security Council last year to pass Resolution 2178, which required UN member states to detain and prosecute foreign fighters crossing their borders.[209] The resolution also pressured members to accelerate counterterrorism information sharing and tighten border controls through more secure travel documents and suspicious-passenger targeting systems.[210] Some countries are making progress, but we believe many have a long way to go.

Key Finding 29: *U.S. defenses against terrorist travel are weakened by glaring and persistent security gaps in foreign countries. This includes insufficient intelligence collection, poor information sharing, lax screening of travelers, inadequate laws for prosecuting terrorists and foreign fighters, and weak border security. We are particularly concerned about gaps in Europe, which has become a major transit pathway for jihadists.*

America cannot stop threats if it cannot see them coming. In the case of terrorist travel, when foreign governments are unable to identify extremists within their own borders or do not share information about them, it increases the odds they will evade our own security systems. Unfortunately, a number of our foreign partners have invested too little in border management and counterterrorism tools, missing critical opportunities to stop the movement of extremists and increasing the risk to the rest of the international community.

When assessing overseas gaps, the Task Force focused primarily on problems in Europe for two reasons. First, most of the Westerners who have gone to fight in Syria and Iraq—including the Americans—transited Europe at some point, with the most common entry point into Syria being Turkey, which straddles Europe and Asia. Second, thousands of Europeans have gone to fight with jihadists, and it is easier for them to travel to the United States on their passports than it is for citizens on most other continents. Thus, European foreign fighters represent a somewhat higher terror travel threat to the United States.

Europe's 26-country Schengen Area is ground zero for the continent's terrorist travel woes. Members of the area have abolished border checkpoints and passport controls to allow anyone inside it to move effortlessly between the many countries. But in addition to helping tourists, the wide-open area has become a boon for terrorists. The European Union (EU) does not have common police or intelligence services, making it easy for violent extremists and foreign fighters to change locations and keep authorities from catching onto them. The assailant behind an attempted terrorist attack in August on a high-speed train from Amsterdam to Paris— Ayoub El Khazzani—is the perfect example. He is suspected of having traveled to link up with extremists in Syria and despite being on several European countries' watchlists, traveled easily between France, Belgium, Austria, and Germany before launching his attack.[211]

Jihadists are well-aware of Europe's security loopholes. An ISIS e-book published this year advises aspiring fighters to start their travel to Syria in tourist hotspots like Spain and Greece—"or any European country"—because authorities are less likely to detect them.[212] Jihadi John, the masked British ISIS fighter responsible for gruesome public beheading videos, reportedly traveled freely through Europe despite being on a terrorist watchlist. Similarly Hayat Boumeddiene, an associate of the Charlie Hebdo terrorists, was known to French police but avoided detection by leaving the country, driving to Spain, and boarding a flight for Turkey. "I had no difficulty getting here," she bragged from Syria in an ISIS-published interview.[213]

The larger concern is that some European extremists might be able to make it to the United States undetected once they have left the battlefield. We have no doubt that European authorities have failed to identify a sizeable number of their citizens who have migrated to Syria and Iraq because there are so many of them and their movements are hard to track in a place like the Schengen Area, with its lax counterterrorism policies. As a result, such individuals are probably not on EU or American terrorist watchlists, allowing them to return to the West under-the-radar.

Many of our foreign partners in Europe, such as the United Kingdom, have sophisticated efforts in place to stop terrorist travel, while others are starting to take more serious action. Terrorist attacks in the streets of Brussels and Paris were a wake-up call, and European authorities are disrupting plots every month, some of which have been planned by returning jihadists. The heightened threat environment has led to a flurry of EU-wide activity to improve security. But we remain concerned some of our partners are not moving quickly enough, allowing terrorist and foreign fighter travel to continue in both directions.

Intelligence Collection and Information Sharing

Much of Europe has slashed defense and intelligence budgets in the decades since the Cold War ended. Those cuts, combined with a surge in cases involving terrorists and homegrown violent extremists, have put serious strain on security services across the continent. Indeed, the Task Force consistently heard concerns that a number of our foreign partners do not have sufficient capabilities needed to identify and track the rising number of terrorists and homegrown violent extremists.[214] This is a real problem. If European security services cannot identify extremists in the first place, then they will be unable to share their biographic information with partners like the United States, and most importantly, detect them when they travel.

A deteriorating threat picture has motivated some countries to take action. In the wake of the Charlie Hebdo attacks, for instance, French Prime Minister Manuel Valls declared the country's "No. 1 priority, the No. 1 requirement" would be "to further reinforce the human and technical resources of intelligence services"; the government has since announced plans for an additional 3,000 counterterrorism professionals.[215] But this does not solve the problem of intra-European cooperation, which is essential when terrorist can so easily move between European countries.

The Task Force found barriers to information sharing to be a problem—within countries, between them, and with the United States. A number of European governments are stymied by legacy bureaucratic stovepipes, turf battles, or strict data privacy laws that prevent collaboration between agencies. Even in major West European capitals, security agencies are often still not well-integrated with border authorities and do not freely share information. We found one top U.S. ally, for instance, did not regularly include border officials in its national security policymaking process, despite serious counterterrorism threats at the country's borders.

EU security officials also expressed concern to the Task Force that continent's intelligence and security services are not always exchanging information with one another. In the 26-country Schengen Area, for example, Country X might share its foreign fighter names with Country Y but not with neighboring Country Z. This creates a security gap since an individual can travel freely anywhere inside the area. EU-wide watchlists were supposed to solve this problem, but officials say member states have been reluctant to place all of their suspects in those databases.

In short, information about foreign fighters is crossing borders less quickly than the extremists themselves. Turkey is an illustrative example. Despite the fact that it is the main transit point into Syria for Westerners, several European countries were still hesitant to share their watchlists of suspected foreign fighters with Turkey, whether for privacy, security, or political reasons. The result is that the Turkish government says it is unable to identify and stop many individuals who might be headed to or from the conflict zone.

U.S. officials have reportedly begun to urge their counterparts in Europe to share all the data they can with Turkish authorities. Some progress has been made. In 2011, Turkey's "no-entry" watchlist only had 280 names; as of July, it contained more than 14,000 names from 94 countries, thanks in large part to information provided by foreign intelligence and security agencies.[216] But with the number of known foreign fighters getting close to 30,000, Turkey is clearly still missing a substantial number of names, some of which foreign partners likely possess but may not have shared.

As far as transatlantic information-sharing goes, we believe counterterrorism exchanges between the United States and Europe have improved considerably in recent years, but some of our partners are still not living up to their obligations, as detailed in Key Finding 8.

Traveler Screening

We are deeply concerned our European allies are not conducting sufficient counterterrorism checks at their borders and airports. Many countries have failed to implement comprehensive watchlisting and screening procedures or do not conduct suspicious traveler "targeting" to find previously unidentified extremists based on travel patterns and other data. These tools are critical tripwires needed to prevent the cross-border movement of violent extremists.

Most alarming is the failure of European states to screen their own citizens against terrorist watchlists when they travel.

Most alarming is the failure of European states to screen their own citizens against terrorist watchlists when they travel. EU rules forbids blanket screening of citizens, meaning most Europeans are not checked for terror ties when they fly into and out of the continent.[217] Border guards are permitted to vet specific individuals who seem suspicious against counterterrorism databases, but only on a "non-systematic" bases.[218] With so many Europeans traveling to fight in Syria, we believe this is a dangerous weakness, which could allow extremists to easily make it back home without being flagged.[219] By comparison, anyone traveling to and from the United States, including U.S. citizens, are screened against counterterrorism databases at multiple points in the journey, from ticket purchase to takeoff.

We are also concerned even more basic screening measures, such as full passport checks, are not happening at European airports and external border crossing. Border guards reportedly screen only 30 percent of EU passports for fraud when citizens depart from or return to the Schengen Area.[220] Most of the time they simply do a quick visual inspections before waiving EU citizens past the checkpoint.[221] This lax security practice is an open invitation to fraud and a glaring security loophole which makes it easier for extremists to sneak into the West on false documents.[222] European leaders pledged at the beginning of this year to do more, but a May report indicated there was no agreement between countries on doing systematic checks on traveler documents; indeed, only one country was doing so.[223]

European authorities have also failed to develop a system for collecting data on air passengers flying into and out of the continent. The combination of airplane manifests and booking information—known as Passenger Name Record (PNR) data[224]—would allow border officers to spot suspicious individuals before they arrive at the airport. U.S. authorities say such tools have been essential for helping them identify previously unknown terrorist suspects and for deciding in a risk-based manner which travelers to send to secondary screening before they even land.

The EU is currently considering a PNR system which, like the United States, would require airlines to share data on passengers entering or exiting the EU for counterterrorism purposes. However, the Task Force is worried such a system will not be approved and fully implemented for years because of the EU's slow bureaucratic movement on the issue.[225] Currently a handful of EU states have developed their own "pilot" PNR systems, but a patchwork of different national systems is a weak substitute for a regional system. Without an EU-wide capability, more violent extremists will slip through the cracks. This, in turn, affects America's security as well.

The lack of a PNR system is not just a European problem. In fact, most countries not only lack PNR systems but do not collect even more basic Advanced Passenger Information (API). While PNR data is more detailed and can be received by authorities when a ticket is purchased, API data is what a passenger submits at check-in, including name, date of birth, and basic flight information. According to a UN report, only one-fourth of countries in the world collect and screen API data before flights in order to identify threats, a serious global gap in efforts to stem terrorist travel.[226] And only 12 of the

UN's 193 member states have API systems which can do passenger risk assessments in near real-time to alert border authorities to terror suspects and potential foreign fighters who may be headed their way.[227]

Turkey, which is not a member of the EU, has grappled with many of the same issues. We are pleased to see Turkish authorities have begun to toughen watchlist screening, including adding thousands of names to its no-entry list in recent months and placing "Risk Analysis Units" (RAUs) at airports and bus stations to detect suspicious travelers. Turkey says these efforts have helped it deport more than 1,300 suspects since the Syrian civil war began, including individuals who have tried multiple times to enter Turkey on the way to join ISIS.

The Task Force is concerned however that other countries may not always be notified by Turkish police when one of their own citizens is turned away at the Turkish border for counterterrorism reasons. Notification is important, as it tips off authorities from the origin country to investigate suspicious individuals once they return. Moreover, even though the RAUs are a step in the right direction, some have questioned whether they are analytically rigorous and whether the officers doing the manual targeting have the tools to conduct effective, risk-based searches of passengers.

We are also concerned that Turkey may not be comprehensively screening all outbound air passengers against national and international terrorist databases and watchlists, as well as travelers at locations like seaports and land border crossings which extremists leaving Syria are increasingly using to avoid scrutiny. Additionally, Turkey still has not implemented its own API / PNR systems. Such capabilities are urgently needed to spot arriving and departing foreign fighters, especially since Turkey is the main transit country to the ISIS safe haven. Officials say they are working on one, but the timeline for implementation is unclear. Despite these areas for improvement, Turkey has come a long way in the past year and is clearly taking steps to tighten security.

Counterterrorism Laws and Prosecutions

We found a number of foreign partners have been slow to update their counterterrorism laws to keep pace with the threat, including several key countries in Europe. Turkey is the most concerning example. Turkish law does not criminalize participation in international terrorism; instead it focuses more narrowly on defining terrorism as a crime against the Turkish state or its people.[228] The State Department believes this "can be an impediment to operational and legal cooperation against global terrorist network," and with thousands of foreign fighters transiting Turkey's territory, the Task Force believes it is indeed an impediment.

Legal inconsistencies on the continent are a systemic problem. Countries like France have made it a crime to join a terrorist group abroad. In contrast, some Nordic countries have not made the law as clear and, therefore, lack the legal tools to prosecute citizens for attempting to become foreign fighters.[229] Sweden, for example, can prosecute individuals for preparing to commit acts of terrorism but does not criminalize the act of training with terrorists or waging war on behalf of a terrorist group.[230] European officials signed a pact in May to synchronize their counterterrorism laws in light of the foreign fighter threat, but it is unclear whether states will treat the move as merely symbolic or act on it decisively.[231]

Some countries in the international community have made legislative improvements since the passage of UN Security Council Resolution 2178, which urged all UN member states to combat foreign fighter travel. Nearly two dozen have updated their laws to better prosecute aspiring and returning foreign fighters, and others are working to do the same.[232] In Europe, Bulgaria is a noteworthy case. The State Department warned last year that Bulgaria "lack[ed] a comprehensive counterterrorism legal framework," but this year the country put forward major terror-related legislation, citing Resolution 2178.[233]

Even with counterterrorism laws on the books, governments have struggled to prosecute extremists, especially when their lawyers have limited experience with terrorism crimes. DOJ has worked to deploy legal experts to some of these countries, such as in the Balkans, where certain states are less equipped to prosecute such cases.[234] However, in other places the problem is making litigation "stick" on appeal. In Sweden for instance, several counterterrorism cases were thrown out last year when judges found the evidence was insufficient to prove suspects would have carried out their plots had they not been intercepted.[235] This is a recurring theme in parts of Europe where judges are less accustomed to hearing terrorism cases or where vague laws make it difficult to prosecute them.

We are also worried a weak European border security posture is increasing the risk of extremists infiltrating the West undetected. The continent faces an unprecedented immigration crisis. In fact, Europe is on track to see nearly double the number of illegal migrants this year than it did in 2014. By year's end, the UN estimates more than 400,000 will have arrived.[236] Most are fleeing the conflict in Syria or instability in North Africa, and they are slipping across land borders or transiting the Mediterranean by boat to reach European border states like Greece or Italy. Once in mainland Europe—and inside the Schengen Area—these refugees can travel freely to the country of their choice to seek asylum.

ISIS has boasted for months that it is using migrant boats as a Trojan Horse to plant operatives into the West,[237] and the EU's border control agency, Frontex, warned this year it was possible extremists were doing so.[238] Not long ago a top EU official confirmed there was information suggesting militants had successfully been smuggled in on these illegal routes.[239] Terrorist exploitation of refugee pathways is not a hypothetical. In May of this year, Italian police arrested a Moroccan man for helping organize the ISIS-linked terrorist attack on Tunisia's Bardo Museum, which resulted in the deaths of more than a dozen Western tourists. The man is believed to have arrived in Italy on a smuggler's boat.[240]

Unfortunately, the European countries where migrants land are not inclined to thoroughly vet them. Under European law, refugees must be stay in the country where they arrive and are registered. Yet many Mediterranean states are already overburdened by large migrant populations drawing on social services and do not want the new arrivals to stay. As a result, border states have an incentive to "look the other way" and let unregistered migrants make their way into the rest of the continent to become another country's problem.

> Nobody checked us upon reaching Italy. No coast guard, no policeman ever asked if we had papers. Nobody registered us, nobody took a photo of us, nobody took our fingerprints, no one asked us who we were.
>
> MUHAMMAD, SYRIAN MIGRANT

"Nobody checked us upon reaching Italy," one Syrian migrant named Muhammad reported. "No coast guard, no policeman ever asked if we had papers. Nobody registered us, nobody took a photo of us, nobody took our fingerprints, no one asked us who we were."[241] The Task Force was disturbed to find such cases were all-too-common—even the norm—in European border states overwhelmed by refugee arrivals.

Some refugees are screened against counterterrorism databases, but the Task Force was told the majority of arrivals are not. Extremists who blend in with these asylum-seekers and make their way onto the continent could easily obtain European passports within a few short years and have visa-free access to the United States. While the scenario is not the likeliest route for terrorist travel, it is certainly possible, especially since terrorist groups have vowed to exploit weaknesses in refugee routes.

The refugee quoted above, Muhammed, is now settled in Germany but warns that others could follow his same path to commit acts of terror. "Any ISIS terrorist could have entered Italy and traveled further into Europe without any problem," he explained. "ISIS members can take their guns and hand grenades with them, because the Italians even never checked any of the luggage."[242] Italian authorities have taken steps to mitigate the danger of terrorist exploitation at their borders, but the system for screening new arrivals is still nowhere near secure.

Governments throughout the region have criticized Mediterranean countries for not showing leadership to tackle the migrant crisis. But Mediterranean states are quick to note they are overwhelmed by the influx of refugees and need more assistance from the rest of Europe, arguing border security should be a shared burden and not just the job of those at the continent's frontiers. Whatever the case, Europe's halting response to the crisis at its borders is a golden opportunity for terrorists and a ticking time-bomb for the West.

As noted above, the Task Force focused primarily on security weaknesses in Europe because of the routes American foreign fighters have taken to the conflict zone in Syria and Iraq, as well as how easy it is for potential European extremist to travel to the United States on their passports. We do not mean to suggest our European partners are failing to confront terrorism and the foreign fighter threat overall, but rather that foundational problems remain and must be addressed with greater urgency. Many countries face steeper challenges when it comes to combating terrorist travel, especially in North Africa and the Middle East. More must be done globally to shine a light on these security deficiencies and collaborate to reconcile them.

Recommendation: The State Department and DHS, in consultation with the intelligence community, should produce a regular report card highlighting the progress of foreign partners in fulfilling their obligations under UN Security Council Resolution 2178 on foreign fighters and underscore areas where partners need improvement. Such reports should be provided to Congress in classified and unclassified form, with the latter being made public. Moreover, they should assess the progress of foreign partners in areas including, but not limited to, intelligence collection, information sharing, traveler screening, legal frameworks, and border security; were possible, these assessments should also incorporate any similar insights on foreign partner capacity released by the UN's Counterterrorism Implementation Task Force Office.

Recommendation: The Administration must continue pressing foreign partners, especially in Europe, to end the patchwork approach to information sharing by including more terrorist and foreign fighter names in regional and international terrorist watchlists—rather than conducting exchanges on a selective, bilateral basis. We understand there are sometimes sensitivities to such sharing, but to the furthest extent possible these partners must move toward universal situational awareness to combat the growing and dynamic terrorist threat. Additionally, the Administration should continue its efforts to make sure foreign governments are sharing appropriate information with Turkish authorities, who are on the frontlines of the foreign fighter migration.

Recommendation: The United States must increase pressure on European partners to begin universally and systematically screening EU-citizen travelers against terrorist watchlists. Moreover, officials should encourage states outside of the EU, especially Turkey, to screen both inbound and outbound travelers against national and international counterterrorism databases to detect possible foreign fighters—at airports, land border crossings, and sea ports.

Recommendation: The EU must quickly approve and implement a regional air passenger targeting system to collect and analyze Passenger Name Record data for counterterrorism purposes. The United States should continue to encourage the EU to move in this direction and, in the meantime, should consider how to provide expanded assistance to EU countries looking to develop their own individual PNR systems, which are a crucial tool for counterterrorism investigations and uncovering previously unidentified extremists. DHS and the State Department should also explore tying VWP participation to a country's ability to conduct PNR vetting.

Recommendation: U.S. authorities should engage in a high-level dialogue with the UN, EU, and relevant non-EU countries on establishing a better systematic process for vetting refugees fleeing North Africa and the conflict in Syria. Regional authorities must be able to ensure the biographic and biometric information of migrants is screened against counterterrorism databases to weed out potential extremists attempting to infiltrate the West.

Recommendation: DHS and the State Department should explore accelerated expansion of their off-the-shelf interdiction capabilities to high-risk countries. Both departments currently offer ready-made hardware and software to help foreign partners conduct watchlisting, screening, and targeting of terrorists and foreign fighters, including the State Department's Personal Identification Secure Comparison and Evaluation System (PISCES) and CBP's Automated Targeting System Global (ATS-G). The provision of these tools should be better coordinated between the two departments, and in the long run such assistance should be provided consistent with priorities established under the Foreign Partner Engagement Plan, a tool the Task Force calls for under Key Finding 32.

Recommendation: For countries unwilling to accept U.S. border screening tools and assistance, DHS and the State Department should consider releasing "open-source" software based on their watchlisting, screening, and targeting tools. This software could be provided to a neutral organization like INTERPOL for distribution and would offer a more limited set of the capabilities than the technology provided directly by the U.S. government. Even with fewer capabilities, an open-source platform would give countries a powerful starting point for developing and deploying their own terrorist interdiction systems at border checkpoints. The Administration should provide Congress with details on how it would implement such a program.

Key Finding 30: *Extremists are using fraudulent passports to travel discretely. However, a third of the international community—including major source countries of foreign fighters—still do not issue fraud-resistant "e-passports," and most countries are still unable to validate the authenticity of "e-passports."*

It is no secret why passport security is critical in the fight against terrorist travel. "For terrorists, travel documents are as important as weapons," the 9/11 Commission noted in its final report.[243] Unsurprisingly, a number of recent foreign fighter suspects have been found using altered passports, fake passports, and even travel documents belonging to siblings in order to sneak into Syria or travel home.[244] Some are even faking their deaths on the battlefield to avoid scrutiny,[245] increasing concerns that fighters might try to come home with a different identity. Responding to concerns, the UN reminded member states last fall that preventing the forgery of identity papers was a key aspect of preventing "the movement of terrorists."[246]

Fraud-resistant "e-passports" are a useful counterterrorism tool, and adoption of them has grown worldwide in recent years, according to the International Civil Aviation Organization (ICAO). These documents are considered more secure because they incorporate a passenger's biometric information, typically via smart card containing the passenger's face, fingerprint, or iris scan data. However, having an e-passport is not enough; the country reading it must be able to confirm it is authentic, too, which is done through ICAO's "public key directory" program. This allows authorities to validate, for instance, that a traveler's fingerprint matches the traveler's passport.

The Task Force was disappointed to find many countries around the world still do not issue e-passports, including key source countries for foreign fighters. In fact, at least 70 governments—or one-third of the international community— do not issue their citizens e-passports.[247] Tunisia is one of the laggards, which is disturbing considering it is the top source country for foreign fighters headed to Syria and Iraq.[248] Without a secure passport requirement, it is easier for Tunisian jihadists to fake their identities, disguise their travel to the conflict zone, or more easily pose as refugees when trying to enter the West. Other countries of concern which lack e-passports include Egypt, Syria, Jordan, Iraq, Yemen, Afghanistan, Pakistan, and more.[249]

Perhaps more worrisome is the fact that the majority of governments in the world cannot definitively read and authenticate e-passports. This is good news for terrorists and foreign fighters traveling on fraudulent documents. Fewer than 25 percent of countries participate in the ICAO system that allows authorities to confirm an e-passport belongs to its holder. Running the document through the system also confirms it was issued by a legitimate authority, has not been altered, and has not been flagged in the lost or stolen passport system.[250] But key transit countries for Western foreign fighters— including Turkey, Greece, and most of the Balkans states—are not part of the ICAO's program and therefore do not have a reliable system to spot falsified e-passports.[251]

Recommendation: DHS should consider requiring all VWP countries to develop the means to validate fraud-resistant e-passports at their borders and airports. This includes participation in ICAO's "public key directory program" which helps border officers confirm a passport belongs to the person holding it. VWP countries will soon be required to issue their citizens e-passports if they are headed to the United States, but that does not mean those countries can actually authenticate such documents at their own border checkpoints. Requiring our partners to do so would make it harder for terrorists and foreign fighters to use fake documents to cross borders—and could keep them further from our own.

Recommendation: DHS, in conjunction with the State Department, should identify other points of leverage to require or encourage non-VWP countries to issue e-passports and to develop the means to read them at their borders and airports, including providing expanded technical assistance to foreign partners to do so.

Key Finding 31: *Many countries do not consistently add information to INTERPOL's databases, and the majority do not screen against INTERPOL databases in real-time at their borders and airports. This is a clear gap in global defenses against terrorist and foreign fighter travel.*

In December 2014, American medical student Sam Neher traveled to Turkey as a tourist and, while on vacation in Istanbul, his passport was stolen. Neher visited the U.S. Consulate, reported the incident, and received a temporary ID, according to a news report.[252] Little did he know, his passport made its way into a secretive trade in fraudulent documents that is thriving in Turkey and Syria. American and European passports are in high demand because traveler's holding them can access many countries without a visa. According to the report, Neher's passport wound up in the hands of ISIS in Syria, a potential tool for the group to send a jihadist abroad.[253]

Stolen passports like Neher's are supposed to be reported to INTERPOL, which maintains a Stolen and Lost Travel Document Database used to keep terrorists and criminals from traveling on stolen IDs. But the Task Force found the system is deeply fragmented. Many governments are inconsistent in reporting their citizens' missing passports to INTERPOL. Even when they do, other countries must screen against the database to see whether a traveler is using the document illegally. Sadly, the majority of countries in the international community have not connected INTERPOL systems to their border posts for agents to screen against them in real-time.[254]

INTERPOL is a voluntary international police organization made up of 190 participating countries, each of which has its own locally run office connected to INTERPOL systems, known as a National Central Bureau (NCB). Like most countries, America's NCB is based in the nation's capital and is run by DHS and DOJ, which manage U.S. access to the organization's extensive criminal and terrorism databases, as well as its lost and stolen passport database.

INTERPOL officials have been pushing member countries for years to use its systems out in the field, especially at border checkpoints.[255] The United States began doing so in the mid-2000s by screening inbound passengers against the police organization's data. The screening was so useful that U.S. authorities extended it nationwide and began using it to screen outbound passenger, visa applicants, and more. The United States now screens more than 400 million people against INTERPOL's databases annually and gets 35,000 "hits" on the system, helping law enforcement catch wanted criminals and spot fake passports.[256] The organization's data has also helped U.S. law enforcement identify hundreds of previously unknown terrorist suspects and foreign fighters, which have been added to watchlists to ensure they do not enter the United States.[257]

But far too few countries are using these systems at the border. In fact, INTERPOL officials have lamented that "only a handful of countries" are checking its lost and stolen passport database before passengers board flights.[258] By some estimates, fewer than 25 percent of INTERPOL members have set up real-time access to its datasets beyond their NCBs.[259] The reasons are varied. Some governments lack the resources to establish connectivity with disparate border posts. Others are held back by internal policy challenges, where the law enforcement agencies with access to INTERPOL do not provide it to the country's immigration agencies. But the result is the same: lackluster use of the system allows more criminals and extremists to travel the world under the radar.

INTERPOL member states are also not consistent in submitting information to the organization's databases. While the United States adds stolen passport numbers in near-real-time to INTERPOL's records, some governments wait days or weeks before uploading a new batch of lost passport numbers, a window which could allow terrorists and smugglers to cross borders with fraudulent IDs. Even some close U.S. allies with sophisticated security screening have had lapses in their reporting to the system.[260] But when reports are made in a timely manner, it can make all the difference. One of the suspects arrested in connection with a terrorist attack this year on tourists in Tunisia was detained in Italy in part because his mother reported her son's passport missing immediately after the attack.[261]

It is especially important for countries close to terrorist safe havens to use INTERPOL's databases. The Task Force found a number of countries along foreign fighter routes to and from the conflict zone have actually improved their use of the system. Bulgaria, for instance, now screens against the organization's databases at the borders, which has allowed it to detect wanted foreign fighters attempting to cross into its territory. Turkey, however, appears to be inconsistent in its use of INTERPOL to screen travelers, an issue which the Task Force hopes the Turkish government will address expeditiously.

Recommendation: The U.S. government should make it a top diplomatic priority to ramp up foreign partner use of INTERPOL systems, including the regular provision of information to the organization's databases, and as a screening mechanism at borders and ports of entry, especially for counterterrorism purposes. The State Department should regularly assess foreign partner use of INTERPOL systems and share its findings with INTERPOL Washington in order to identify avenues for promoting and enhancing the utilization of these systems.

Recommendation: INTERPOL Washington should be further empowered to deliver assistance to foreign partners who are not fully utilizing the system, whether independently or through a program established out of INTERPOL's headquarters in France. Specifically, INTERPOL Washington should focus on transferring its knowledge, expertise, and systems to high-risk terror-transit countries. The Administration should submit a proposal to Congress to enable INTERPOL Washington to deliver this more robust capacity-building assistance among select member countries, as identified in consultation with interagency partners and with respect to a government-wide Foreign Partner Engagement Plan (see the recommendation under Key Finding 32).

Recommendation: DHS should require VWP countries to screen travelers crossing their borders against all INTERPOL systems, including the Lost and Stolen Passport Database and notices of wanted individuals, including terrorist and foreign fighter suspects.[262] A number VWP countries—whose citizens can travel easily to our country—do not use these tools in real-time at their borders or airports, a security loophole which makes it easier for extremists to travel and increases the chances they could get to the United States undetected.

Recommendation: In conjunction with the State Department, DHS and DOJ should identify other forms of assistance which might be leveraged to require non-VWP countries to use INTERPOL more comprehensively.

Key Finding 32: *U.S. departments and agencies have spent billions of dollars to help foreign partners improve their terror-travel defenses, but there is no strategy to make sure assistance is coordinated and goes to the highest-risk countries. The lack of a government-wide engagement plan results in greater risk of overlap, waste, and duplication between programs.*

In the years since 9/11, the United States has spent considerable time and money to help our allies build the capacity to stop terrorist travel. We have done this by sharing our expertise and best practices. In some cases we have provided travel screening equipment and systems directly to our partners. These efforts have been designed to push our defenses outward and to stop threats earlier.

Multiple U.S. departments and agencies work with foreign partners on these issues. The State Department, for instance, runs the Terrorist Interdiction Program which provides border control hardware and software—including watchlisting tools—to other countries. Around 200 border checkpoints around the world are now tied to the program, which has helped successfully catch terrorists trying to cross borders.[263] DHS's Customs and Border Protection (CBP) provides a similar tool to foreign partners called Automated Targeting System – Global (ATS-G), which can be used to conduct passenger risk assessments in advance of arriving flights to weed out terrorist suspects and foreign fighters. Agencies also provide their expertise. For example, DOJ's Overseas Prosecutorial Development Assistance and Training (OPDAT) program assists prosecutors and judicial personnel in foreign countries with strengthening counterterrorism laws and prosecuting violent extremists.

The Task Force found however that the proliferation of assistance programs has increased the potential for overlap, waste, and duplication among agencies.

The Task Force found however that the proliferation of assistance programs has increased the potential for overlap, waste, and duplication among agencies. GAO highlighted similar concerns in 2011. For example, they discovered that seven different offices or components across the federal government were providing training to foreign officials on how to recognize fraudulent travel documents.[264] In one instance, two U.S. government agencies in Pakistan even scheduled fraud-detection training sessions in the same month without knowing it. One had ample funding but no Pakistani officials had enrolled in the class; the other had a full student roster but lacked necessary funding.[265]

We are concerned departments and agencies are still not adequately coordinating their efforts. For instance, the Task Force spoke to two separate agencies providing counterterrorism screening systems to foreign partners, yet neither could readily identify the countries in which the other operated. We were also unable to find overarching strategic guidance for coordinating U.S. assistance to combat terrorist travel. One agency claimed to be using a risk-based priority list, ranking countries that needed assistance the most because of security gaps. But those efforts were only begun recently and officials declined to provide supporting data. More than other types of aid, the lack of a high-level strategy for terrorist interdiction assistance is concerning given the urgency of the problem.

> **Recommendation:** The Administration should produce an annual Foreign Partner Engagement Plan as part of a National Strategy to Combat Terror Travel (see Key Finding 1, where the Task Force calls for the Strategy). The Plan should be coordinated with all relevant agencies and must prioritize engagement and assistance based on—among other criteria—foreign partner intelligence capabilities, information-sharing, travel screening, border security, counterterrorism laws, prosecutorial capacity, and related areas. As part of the development of the Plan, agencies should conduct an audit of current initiatives and spending on terrorist-travel related assistance to foreign partners to identify areas for adjustment to align with risk-based priorities. Moreover, the Plan should be provided in conjunction with the President's Budget submission to Congress to ensure priorities are aligned with resource requests.

APPENDIX I: TASK FORCE ACTIVITY

This list includes activities conducted by Members and/or staff of the Task Force; however, the listing is partial and does not include all activities, meetings, and other consultations conducted during the course of the Task Force's review.

Official Member Briefings

Terrorist Watchlisting and Foreign Fighters (March 2015)
Briefers: National Counterterrorism Center

Foreign Partner Information Sharing and Watchlist Enhancements (April 2015)
Briefers: Federal Bureau of Investigation's Terrorist Screening Center

Interagency Programs to Counter Domestic Radicalization (April 2015)
Briefers: Department of Homeland Security, Department of Justice, Federal Bureau of Investigation, National Counterterrorism Center

Site Visit: National Counterterrorism Center (April 2015)
Briefers: National Counterterrorism Center

Site Visit: Washington Regional Threat Analysis Center (April 2015)
Briefers: Center leadership and State and local law enforcement

Counter-Messaging Terrorist Propaganda (May 2015)
Briefers: Department of State

INTERPOL Efforts to Counter Terrorist and Foreign Fighter Travel (June 2015)
Briefers: INTERPOL Washington

Preventing Terrorist Exploitation of Visa-Free Travel Routes to America (June 2015)
Briefers: Department of Homeland Security, Department of State

Online Counterterrorism Operations (June 2015)[263]
Briefers: Federal Bureau of Investigation

Extremists' Use of "Dark Space" (June 2014)[264]
Briefers: Federal Bureau of Investigation

Immigration Screening and Passport Revocations to Stop Terrorist Travel (June 2015)
Briefers: Department of Homeland Security, Department of State
Intelligence Information Sharing (June 2015)
Briefers: Office of the Director of National Intelligence

Site Visit: Joint Terrorism Task Force – Washington (June 2015)
Briefers: Federal Bureau of Investigation

Homeland Security Advisory Council: Interim Report on Foreign Fighters (July 2015)
Briefers: Homeland Security Advisory Council

Overseas U.S. Diplomatic Efforts to Obstruct Foreign Fighter Flows (July 2015)
Briefers: Department of State

Arrest and Prosecution of U.S. Foreign Fighter Suspects (July 2015)
Briefers: Department of Justice

Official Staff Briefings

Department of Defense (1)
Department of Homeland Security (6)
Department of Justice (2)
Department of State (2)
Federal Bureau of Investigation (5)
Government Accountability Office (7)
INTERPOL Washington (2)
National Counterterrorism Center (1)
Other Intelligence Community (3)

Iraq
U.S. Embassy
Meeting with Prime Minister Abadi
Meeting with Deputy Prime Minister Zebari
Meeting with Speaker Jabouri

Israel
U.S. Embassy
Meeting with Prime Minister Netanyahu
Meeting with Defense Minister Yaalon
Meeting with Deputy Foreign Minister Hanegbi

Turkey
U.S. Embassy
Ministry of Foreign Affairs
Ministry of Interior
Hollings Center for International Dialogue
Istanbul Airport Security Brief

Germany
U.S. Embassy
Ministry of Interior
Interior Committee, Bundestag

Belgium
U.S. Embassy and Mission to the European Union (EU)
Meeting with Interior Minister Jambon
EU Counterterrorism Officials
NATO Headquarters
Transatlantic Policy Network

France
U.S. Embassy
French Counterterrorism Officials
INTERPOL

Official Staff Travel

Greece
U.S. Embassy
Ministry of Public Order and Citizen Protection
Civil Aviation Authority
Hellenic Coast Guard
Hellenic Police

Turkey
U.S. Embassy
Ministry of Foreign Affairs
NATO
Izmir Port Security
EU Counterterrorism Officials
Turkish National Police

Italy
U.S. Embassy
Ministry of Foreign Affairs
Ministry of Interior
Catania Refugee Processing Center
International Organization for Migration
UN High Commissioner for Refugees

Other Task Force Meetings and Consultations

Members and staff also met with state and local representatives, former government officials, think tanks, academics, professional organizations, and other individuals during the course of the review. Though they are not listed by name, the Task Force is grateful for the valuable input it received and the contributions of these individuals and organizations.

APPENDIX II: AMERICAN FOREIGN FIGHTER ASPIRANTS & RECRUITS

Name	Age[265]	Gender	State
Abdella Ahmad Tounisi	21	M	IL
Abdi Nur	20	M	MN
Abdifatah Aden		M	OH
Abdirahmaan Muhumed	29	M	MN
Abdirahman Sheik Mohamud	23	M	OH
Abdirahman Yasin Daud	21	M	MN
Abdullah Ramo Pazara		M	MO
Abdullahi Yusuf	18	M	MN
Abdurasul Juraboev	23	M	NY
Adam Dandach	20	M	CA
Adnan Abdihamid Farah	19	M	MN
Ahmad Abousamra	32	M	MA
Akba Jihad Jordan	22	M	NC
Akhror Saidakhmetov	19	M	NY
Amir Farouq Ibrahim	32	M	PA
Arafat Nagi	44	M	NY
Asher Abid Khan	20	M	TX
Avin Marsalis Brown	21	M	NC
Basit Javed	29	M	NC
Bilal Abood	37	M	TX
Colorado Teenager #1	15	F	CO
Colorado Teenager #2	15	F	CO
Colorado Teenager #3	17	F	CO
Donald Ray Morgan	44	M	NC
Douglas McArthur McCain	33	M	CA
Eric Harroun	30	M	AZ
Guled Ali Omar	20	M	MN
"H.M."		M	MN
Hamza Naj Ahmed	19	M	MN
Hanad Abdullahi Mohallim	18	M	MN
Hanad Mustafe Musse	19	M	MN
Hasan Edmonds	22	M	IL
Hoda	20	F	AL
Jaelyn Delshaun Young	20	F	MS
Joshua Van Haften	34	M	WI

Keonna Thomas	30	F	PA
Leon Nathan Davis	37	M	GA
Michael Wolfe	23	M	TX
Mohamad Saeed Kodaimati	24	M	CA
Mohamed Abdihamid Farah	21	M	MN
Mohammad Hamzah Khan	19	M	IL
Mohamud Mohamed Mohamud	20	M	MN
Moner Abu-Salha	22	M	FL
Muhammad Oda Dakhlalla	22	M	MS
Muhanad Badawi	24	M	CA
Nader Elhuzayel	24	M	CA
Nader Saadeh	20	M	NJ
Nicholas Teausant	20	M	CA
Nicole Lynn Mansfield	33	F	MI
Nihad Rosic	26	M	NY
"S.R.G."		M	TX
Samuel Rahamin Topaz	21	M	NJ
Shannon Maureen Conley	19	F	CO
Sinh Vinh Ngo Nguyen	24	M	CA
Tairod Nathan Webster Pugh	47	M	NJ
Yusra Ismail	20	F	MN
Yusuf Jama	21	M	MN
Zacharia Yusuf Abdurahman	19	M	MN

APPENDIX III: ABBREVIATIONS

API	Advanced Passenger Information
AQI	al Qaeda in Iraq
ATS-G	U.S. Customs and Border Protection's Automated Targeting System Global
CBP	U.S. Customs and Border Protection
CSCC	Center for Strategic Counterterrorism Communications
CTAB	Department of Homeland Security's Counterterrorism Advisory Board
DHS	Department of Homeland Security
DNI	Director of National Intelligence
DOJ	Department of Justice
ESTA	Electronic System for Travel Authorization
EU	European Union
FBI	Federal Bureau of Investigation
FEMA	Federal Emergency Management Agency
GAO	Government Accountability Office
HSPD-6	Homeland Security Presidential Directive 6
ICAO	International Civil Aviation Organization
ICE	Immigration and Customs Enforcement
ISIS	Islamic State of Iraq and Syria (also Islamic State of Iraq and the Levant)
INTERPOL	International Criminal Police Organization
JTTF	Federal Bureau of Investigation's Joint Terrorism Task Force
NCB	National Central Bureau
NCTC	National Counterterrorism Center
NGO	Non-Governmental Organization
OPDAT	The Department of Justice's Overseas Prosecutorial Development Assistance and Training
PATRIOT	Pre-Adjudicated Threat Recognition and Intelligence Operations Team
PISCES	Personal Identification Secure Comparison and Evaluation System
PNR	Passenger Name Record
RAU	Risk Analysis Unit
TSA	Transportation Security Administration
TSDB	Terrorist Screening Database
UN	United Nations
VSP	Visa Security Program
VSU	Visa Security Unit
VWP	Visa Waiver Program
WORDE	World Organization for Resource Development and Education

APPENDIX IV: ENDNOTES

1 Barbara Starr, "'A Few Dozen Americans' in ISIS Ranks," CNN, July 15, 2015, http://www.cnn.com/2015/07/15/politics/isis-american-recruits/.

2 Ibid.

3 See Key Finding 1.

4 The Committee was given discretion to make technical, grammatical, and other conforming changes prior to release.

5 Kimiko De Freytas-Tamura, "Junaid Hussain, ISIS Recruiter, Reported Killed in Airstrike," The New York Times, August 27, 2015, http://www.nytimes.com/2015/08/28/world/middleeast/junaid-hussain-islamic-state-recruiter-killed.html?_r=0; Mark Schliebs, "American Drone Expunges Aussie-Linked Islamic Terrorist," August 28, 2015, http://www.theaustralian.com.au/in-depth/terror/american-drone-expunges-aussie-linked-islamic-state-terrorist/story-fnpdbcmu-1227501807553?sv=3c3f680b59882e16aa53c911d5b7047d.

6 John Bacon, "Ohio Man Accused of Planning U.S. Terror Strike," USA Today, April 16, 2015, http://www.usatoday.com/story/news/nation/2015/04/16/ohio-indicted-islamic-state-terrorism/25879443/.

7 See "The Danger of Foreign Fighters" subsection of this report for a list of recent returnee attacks.

8 Ken Dilanian, Zeina Karam, and Bassem Mroue, Associated Press, "Pummeled in Its Capital, Islamic State Group Still Hanging Tough across Iraq and Syria," U.S. News, July 31, 2015, http://www.usnews.com/news/politics/articles/2015/07/31/despite-bombing-islamic-state-is-no-weaker-than-a-year-ago.

9 Ibid.

10 U.S. Congress. Majority Staff of the House Homeland Security Committee. Terror Threat Snapshot: September 2015, http://homeland.house.gov/sites/homeland.house.gov/files/documents/Complete%20September%20Terror%20Threat%20Snapshot.pdf. 11 Ibid.

12 Brian Michael Jenkins, "When Jihadis Come Marching Home: The Terrorist Threat Posed by Westerners Returning from Syria and Iraq," Perspectives. RAND Corporation, 2014, 12-13, http://www.rand.org/content/dam/rand/pubs/perspectives/PE100/PE130-1/RAND_PE130-1.pdf.

13 House Committee on Homeland Security, Worldwide Threats to the Homeland: Hearing Before the Committee on Homeland Security, 113th Cong., 2nd sess., September 17, 2014, http://www.gpo.gov/fdsys/pkg/CHRG-113hhrg93367/html/CHRG-113hhrg93367.htm.

14 Kareem Fahim and Hwaida Saad, "A Faceless Teenage Refugee Who Helped Ignite Syria's War," The New York Times, February 08, 2013, http://www.nytimes com/2013/02/09/world/middleeast/a-faceless-teenage-refugee-who-helped-ignite-syrias-war.html?_r=2.

15 Lucy Rodgers, David Gritten, James Offer, and Patrick Asare, "Syria: The Story of the Conflict," BBC News, March 12, 2015, http://www.bbc.com/news/world-middle-east-26116868.

16 Thomas Hegghammer and Aaron Y. Zelin, "How Syria's Civil War Became a Holy Crusade," Foreign Affairs, October 15, 2014, https://www.foreignaffairs.com/articles/middle-east/2013-07-03/how-syrias-civil-war-became-holy-crusade.

17 Ibid.

18 Thomas Hegghammer, "Syria's Foreign Fighters," Foreign Policy, December 9, 2013, http://foreignpolicy.com/2013/12/09/syrias-foreign-fighters/.

19 Ibid.

20 Aaron Y. Zelin, "Up to 11,000 Foreign Fighters in Syria; Steep Rise among Western Europeans," ICSR Insight, December 17, 2013, http://icsr.info/2013/12/icsr-insight-11000-foreign-fighters-syria-steep-rise-among-western-europeans/.

21 Ibid.

22 Eric Schmitt, "U.S. Says Dozens of Americans Have Sought to Join Rebels in Syria," The New York Times, November 20, 2013, http://www.nytimes.com/2013/11/21/world/middleeast/us-says-dozens-of-americans-have-sought-to-join-rebels-in-syria.html.

23 Christopher M. Blanchard, Carla E. Humud, Kenneth Katzman, and Matthew C. Weed, The "Islamic State" Crisis and U.S. Policy (CRS Report No. R43612) (Washington, DC: Congressional Research Service, 2015), http://fas.org/sgp/crs/mideast/R43612.pdf.

24 Barak Mendelsohn, "After Disowning ISIS, Al Qaeda Is Back On Top," Foreign Affairs, February 13, 2014, https://www.foreignaffairs.com/articles/middle-east/2014-02-13/after-disowning-isis-al-qaeda-back-top.

25 Brett McGurk, Al-Qaeda's Resurgence in Iraq: A Threat to U.S. Interests: Hearing before the House Foreign Affairs Committee, testimony, 113th Cong., 2nd sess., February 5, 2014, http://www.state.gov/p/nea/rls/rm/221274.htm.

26 "Isis Rebels Declare 'Islamic State' in Iraq and Syria," BBC News, June 30, 2014, http://www.bbc.com/news/world-middle-east-28082962.

27 Paul Cruickshank, "Al Qaeda in Yemen Rebukes ISIS - CNN.com," CNN, November 21, 2014, http://www.cnn.com/2014/11/21/world/meast/al-qaeda-yemen-isis/.

28 U.S. Department of Justice. Office of Public Affairs. Attorney General Holder Urges International Effort to Confront Threat of Syrian Foreign Fighters, July 8, 2014, http://www.justice.gov/opa/pr/attorney-general-holder-urges-international-effort-confront-threat-syrian-foreign-fighters.

29 Daniel L. Byman and Jeremy Shapiro, "Managing the Foreign Fighter Threat," The Brookings Institution, January 14, 2015, http://www.brookings.edu/blogs/markaz/posts/2015/01/14-byman-shapiro-foreign-fighters.

30 UN Department of Public Information, "Security Council Unanimously Adopts Resolution Condemning Violent Extremism, Underscoring Need to Prevent Travel, Support for Foreign Terrorist Fighters," SC/11580, September 24, 2014, http://www.un.org/press/en/2014/sc11580.doc.htm.

31 Keith Sullivan and Karla Adam, "Hoping to Create a New Society, the Islamic State Recruits Entire Families," Washington Post, December 24, 2014, https://www.washingtonpost.com/world/national-security/hoping-to-create-a-new-homeland-the-islamic-state-recruits-entire-families/2014/12/24/dbffceec-8917-11e4-8ff4-fb93129c-9c8b_story.html.

32 Ibid.

33 Ibid.

34 U.S. Department of Defense, "Special Report: Inherent Resolve," Operation Inherent Resolve: Targeted Operations Against ISIL Terrorists, accessed September 19, 2015, http://www.defense.gov/News/Special-Reports/0814_Inherent-Resolve.

35 Matthew G. Olsen, Worldwide Threats to the Homeland: Hearing Before the Committee on Homeland Security, 113th Cong., 2nd sess., September 17, 2014, http://docs.house.gov/meetings/HM/HM00/20140917/102616/HHRG-113-HM00-Wstate-OlsenM-20140917.pdf.

36 Jeff Seldin, "More Foreign Fighters in Iraq, Syria," VOA, December 24, 2014, http://www.voanews.com/content/estimates-rising-of-foreign-fighters-in-iraq-syria/2572994.html.

37 Nicholas J. Rasmussen, Countering Violent Islamist Extremism: The Urgent Threat of Foreign Fighters and Homegrown Terror: Hearing before the House Committee on Homeland Security, 114th Cong., 1st sess., February 11, 2015, http://docs.house.gov/meetings/HM/HM00/20150211/102901/HHRG-114-HM00-Wstate-RasmussenN-20150211.pdf.

38 Using U.S. government public estimates, the overall number has risen from 7,000-plus in July of last year to 25,000-plus today.

39 Homeland Security Committee. Terror Threat Snapshot: September 2015.

40 Dilanian, Karam, and Mroue, AP, "Islamic State Hanging Tough."

41 Laura Smith-Spark and Noisette Martel, "U.S. Official: 10,000 ISIS Fighters Killed in 9 Months," CNN, June 3, 2015, http://www.cnn.

com/2015/06/03/middleeast/isis-conflict/.

42 Eric Schmitt and David Kirk Patrick, "Islamic State Sprouting Limbs Beyond Its Base," The New York Times, February 14, 2015, http://www.nytimes.com/2015/02/15/world/middleeast/islamic-state-sprouting-limbs-beyond-mideast.html.

43 Ibid.

44 Jack Moore, "5,000 Foreign Fighters Flock to Libya as ISIS Call for Jihadists," Newsweek, March 3, 2015, http://europe.newsweek.com/5000-foreign-fighters-flock-libya-isis-call-jihadists-310948.

45 Ibid.

46 Everett Rosenfeld, "Fear Grows in Europe as ISIS Comes to Libya," CNBC, February 20, 2015, http://www.cnbc.com/2015/02/20/islamic-state-terrorism-fear-grows-in-europe-as-isis-comes-to-libya.html.

47 Seth G. Jones, "Expanding the Caliphate," Foreign Affairs, June 11, 2015, https://www.foreignaffairs.com/articles/afghanistan/2015-06-11/expanding-caliphate.

48 Emma Graham-Harrison, "Taliban Fears over Young Recruits Attracted to Isis in Afghanistan," The Guardian, May 7, 2015, http://www.theguardian.com/world/2015/may/07/taliban-young-recruits-isis-afghanistan-jihadis-islamic-state.

49 Task Force staff briefing, March 2015.

50 Geoff Earle, "Western ISIS Fighters Are the Most Brutal: Defector," New York Post, September 29, 2014, http://nypost.com/2014/09/29/western-isis-fighters-are-the-most-brutal-defector/.

51 Soaud Mekhennet and Adam Goldman, "'Jihadi John': Islamic State Killer Is Identified as Londoner Mohammed Emwazi," Washington Post, February 26, 2015, https://www.washingtonpost.com/world/national-security/jihadi-john-the-islamic-state-killer-behind-the-mask-is-a-young-londoner/2015/02/25/d6dbab16-bc43-11e4-bdfa-b8e8f594e6ee_story.html.

52 Omar Wahid, "Jihadi John - 'I Will Go Back to Britain... and Will Carry on Cutting Heads Off': In a Chilling New Video, Man Said to Be Hooded Butcher Vows to Return... and Murder All Unbelievers," Daily Mail Online, August 22, 2015, http://www.dailymail.co.uk/news/article-3207366/Jihadi-John-Britain-carry-cutting-heads-chilling-new-video-man-said-hooded-butcher-beheaded-two-British-hostages-vows-come-home-murder-unbelievers.html.

53 Peter Neumann, "War on Two Fronts: Perceptions on the Fight against the Islamic State," The Finnish Institute of International Affairs, October 29, 2014, http://www.fiia.fi/en/event/702/war_on_two_fronts/.

54 McGurk, Al-Qaeda's Resurgence in Iraq.

55 Peter Bergen, "The All-American Al Qaeda Suicide Bomber," CNN, July 31, 2014, http://www.cnn.com/2014/07/31/opinion/bergen-american-al-qaeda-suicide-bomber-syria/.

56 Meg Wagner, "Video: American Suicide Bomber in Syria Threatens U.S.," NY Daily News, July 30, 2014, http://www.nydailynews.com/news/world/american-suicide-bomber-syria-threatens-video-article-1.1885341.

57 Suman Varandani, "About 100 Germans Killed Fighting Alongside ISIS In Iraq And Syria Since 2012, German Interior Minister Says," International Business Times, August 24, 2015, http://www.ibtimes.com/about-100-germans-killed-fighting-alongside-isis-iraq-syria-2012-german-interior-2064892.

58 The study was based on an analysis of Western returnees from 1990 to 2010 who had joined insurgencies in places like Afghanistan and Somalia. See: Thomas Hegghammer, "Should I Stay or Should I Go? Explaining Variation in Western Jihadists Choice between Domestic and Foreign Fighting," American Political Science Review, February 2013, doi: 10.1017/S0003055412000615.

59 Ibid.

60 These arrests are in addition to the dozens of Americans arrested this year either attempting to travel to Syria or engaging in support or plotting inspired by ISIS.

61 United States of America v. Abdirahman Sheik Mohamud, April 16, 2015, http://www.justice.gov/sites/default/files/opa/press-releases/attachments/2015/04/16/mohamud_indictment.pdf.

62 Ibid.

63 While Nagi is not a Syria returnee—as he does not appear he crossed from Turkey into the conflict zone—his case is nevertheless emblematic of radicalized individuals who come back and attempt to recruit others to join the group. See: Lou Michel, "Accused ISIS Recruiter Had Threatened to Behead Daughter, Sources Say," The Buffalo News, July 29, 2015, http://www.buffalonews.com/city-region/lackawanna/accused-isis-recruiter-had-threatened-to-behead-daughter-sources-say-20150729%20.

64 The security of the Visa Waiver Program is discussed elsewhere in the Task Force's report, especially in Key Finding 23.

65 Gilles De Kerchove et al., "Rehabilitation and Reintegration of Returning Foreign Terrorist Fighters," The Washington Institute for Near East Policy, February 23, 2015, http://www.washingtoninstitute.org/policy-analysis/view/rehabilitation-and-reintegration-of-returning-foreign-terrorist-fighters.

66 This list is not comprehensive and also does not reflect Islamist terror plots by returnees from other jihadist safe havens, such as Afghanistan, Pakistan, and Yemen. The Charlie Hebdo attacks, for instance, were plotted by suspects alleged to have trained in Yemen.

67 "Arrested French Jihadist 'Instructed' to Attack Concert," France 24, September 18, 2015, http://www.france24.com/en/20150918-france-jihadist-arrested-terrorist-attack-plot-concert.

68 "Suspected Train Gunman 'known to French Intelligence'," France 24, August 23, 2015, http://www.france24.com/en/20150822-france-train-attack-suspected-gunman-known-french-intelligence-syria.

69 Rick Lyman, "Kosovo Charges 5 People in Plot to Poison Water," The New York Times, July 12, 2015, http://www.nytimes.com/2015/07/13/world/europe/kosovo-charges-5-people-in-plot-to-poison-water.html.

70 Chris Stephen, "Tunisia Gunman Trained in Libya at Same Time as Bardo Museum Attackers," The Guardian, June 30, 2015, http://www.theguardian.com/world/2015/jun/30/tunisia-beach-attack-seifeddine-rezgui-libya-bardo-museum-attackers.

71 "Saudi Arabia Arrest 93 Terror Suspects, Foils Car Bomb Plot on U.S. Embassy," Fox News, April 29, 2015, http://www.foxnews.com/world/2015/04/29/saudi-arabia-arrest-3-terror-suspects-foils-car-bomb-plot-on-us-embassy/.

72 Bacon, "Ohio Man Accused of Planning U.S. Terror Strike."

73 Duncan Gardham, "British Double Agent 'plotted to Kill His MI5 Handler and Attack UK' after Infiltrating Jihadist Group in Syria," Daily Mail Online, March 28, 2015, http://www.dailymail.co.uk/news/article-3016480/British-double-agent-plotted-kill-MI5-handler-attack-UK-infiltrating-jihadist-group-Syria.html.

74 Faith Karimi, Tim Lister, and Greg Botelho, "2 Suspects in Tunisia Attack Trained in Libya," CNN, March 20, 2015, http://www.cnn.com/2015/03/20/africa/tunisia-museum-attack/.

75 Michele Mandel, "Man Accused of U.S. Consulate/Bay St. Bomb Plot to Be Deported," Ottawa Sun, June 5, 2015, http://www.ottawasun.com/2015/06/05/man-accused-of-us-consulatebay-st-bomb-plot-to-be-deported.

76 Yuksel Temel, "Intelligence Uncovers ISIS Plot to Attack Consulates," Daily Sabah, January 25, 2015, http://www.dailysabah.com/nation/2015/01/25/intelligence-uncovers-isis-plot-to-attack-consulates.

77 Matthew Dalton, "Belgium Antiterror Raid Leaves Two Suspects Dead," The Wall Street Journal, January 15, 2015, http://www.wsj.com/articles/belgium-antiterror-raid-leaves-two-dead-official-says-1421350264.

78 Kevin Rawlinson, "Jewish Museum Shooting Suspect Is 'Islamic State Torturer'" The Guardian, September 6, 2014, http://www.theguardian.com/world/2014/sep/06/jewish-museum-shooting-suspect-islamic-state-torturer-brussels-syria.

79 Ben McPartland, "Several 'planned Terrorist Attacks' Foiled in France," The Local France, November 03, 2014, http://www.thelocal.fr/20141103/terrorist-attacks-foiled-in-france.

80 Mary Anne Weaver, "Her Majesty's Jihadists," The New York Times, April 14, 2015, http://www.nytimes.com/2015/04/19/magazine/her-majestys-jihadists.html.

81 Jenkins, "When Jihadis Come Marching Home," 5 – 6. http://www.rand.org/content/dam/rand/pubs/perspectives/PE100/PE130-1/RAND_PE130-1.pdf.

82 Aryn Baker, "How ISIS Is Recruiting Women Around the World," Time Inc., September 6, 2014, http://time.com/3276567/how-isis-is-recruiting-women-from-around-the-world/.

83 "Health Care in the [Caliphate]," Dabiq, no. 9, 25-26, http://media.clarionproject.org/files/islamic-state/isis-isil-islamic-state-magazine-issue%2B9-they-plot-and-allah-plots-sex-slavery.pdf.

84 Ibid.

85 Natalie Andrews and Felicia Schwartz, "Islamic State Pushes Social-Media Battle With West," The Wall Street Journal, August 22, 2014, http://www.wsj.com/articles/isis-pushes-social-media-battle-with-west-1408725614.

86 Ruth Pollard, "Islamic State Propaganda: What the West Doesn t Understand" The Sydney Morning Herald, July 9, 2015, http://www.smh.com.au/world/islamic-state-propaganda-what-the-west-doesnt-understand-20150708-gi86qu.html.

87 Evan Perez, Pamela Brown, and Jim Sciutto, "Texas Attacker Had Private Convos with Known Terrorists," CNN, May 7, 2015, http://www.cnn.com/2015/05/07/politics/fbi-warning-elton-simpson-cartoon-event-attack/index.html.

88 House Homeland Security Committee. Terror Threat Snapshot: September 2015.

89 Starr, "'A Few Dozen Americans' in ISIS Ranks."

90 The overwhelming majority of individuals reviewed were U.S. person; in other words, they were U.S. citizens or legal permanent residents of the United States. Only several cases concerned subjects with other kinds of immigration status, e.g. visa overstays or refugees.

91 While we assessed some classified information related to these cases, we strongly urge the Administration to conduct a full end-to-end review of all U.S. foreign fighter cases, recommended as part of Key Finding 2 in this report.

92 Michael Tarm, "Chicago-area Teen Latest Snared in Website Traps," Yahoo! News, April 23, 2013, http://news.yahoo.com/chicago-area-teen-latest-snared-website-traps-195908623.html.

93 Ibid.

94 Schmitt, "U.S. Says Dozens of Americans Have Sought to Join Rebels in Syria."

95 Reuters, "Fewer than 100 Americans Probed for Fighting in Syria, Iraq: U.S. Attorney General," Business Insider, July 08, 2014, http://www.businessinsider.com/r-fewer-than-100-americans-probed-for-fighting-in-syria-iraq-us-attorney-general-2014-08.

96 Barbara Starr, "'A Few Dozen Americans' in ISIS Ranks," CNN, July 15, 2015, http://www.cnn.com/2015/07/15/politics/isis-american-recruits/.

97 "Arrest Demonstrates Influence of Online Terrorist Materials," Anti-Defamation League (Blog), March 20, 2014, http://blog.adl.org/extremism/arrest-demonstrates-influence-of-online-terrorist-materials.

98 Of the aspiring U.S. foreign fighters in our sample, nine (15 percent) were women. If applied to the 250-plus estimate of total Americans who have traveled or attempted to travel, you get a prediction of around 38 females.

99 U.S. Department of Justice. Office of Public Affairs. Philadelphia Woman Arrested for Attempting to Provide Material Support to ISIL, April 3, 2015, http://www.justice.gov/opa/pr/philadelphia-woman-arrested-attempting-provide-material-support-isil.

100 Evan Perez and Shimon Prokupecz, "ISIS Arrests Highlight Role of American Recruiter," CNN, April 20, 2015, http://www.cnn.com/2015/04/20/politics/isis-minnesota-arrests-abdi-nur/.

101 U.S. Department of Justice. Office of Public Affairs. Columbus, Ohio, Man Charged with Providing Material Support to Terrorists, April 16, 2015, http://www.justice.gov/opa/pr/columbus-ohio-man-charged-providing-material-support-terrorists.

102 Ibid.

103 Starr, "'A Few Dozen Americans' in ISIS Ranks."

104 U S. Department of Justice, Columbus, Ohio, Man Charged with Providing Material Support to Terrorists.

105 Shimon Prokupecz, "3 Denver Teens Back Home after Failed Trip to Syria," CNN, October 23, 2014, http://www.cnn.com/2014/10/21/us/colorado-teens-syria-odyssey/.

106 Ibid.

107 U.S. Department of Justice. Federal Bureau of Investigation. Office of Public Affairs. Six Minnesota Men Charged with Conspiracy to Provide Material Support to the Islamic State of Iraq and the Levant: Four Defendants Arrested in Minneapolis; Two Arrested in San Diego, April 20, 2015, https://www.fbi.gov/minneapolis/press-releases/2015/six-minnesota-men-charged-with-conspiracy-to-provide-material-support-to-the-islamic-state-of-iraq-and-the-levant.

108 Michael Martinez, Ana Cabrera, and Sara Weisfeldt, "Colorado Woman Gets 4 Years for Wanting to Join ISIS," CNN, January 24, 2015, http://www.cnn.com/2015/01/23/us/colorado-woman-isis-sentencing/.

109 Ibid.

110 Alessandria Masi, "ISIS Recruiting Westerners: How The 'Islamic State' Goes After Non-Muslims And Recent Converts In The West," International Business Times, September 08, 2014, http://www.ibtimes.com/isis-recruiting-westerners-how-islamic-state-goes-after-non-muslims-recent-converts-west-1680076.

111 Ibid.

112 Ibid.

113 Dustin Volz, "FBI Director: ISIS Is Relying on Encryption to Recruit Americans and Order Killings," National Journal, July 8, 2015, http://www.nationaljournal.com/tech/fbi-director-isis-is-relying-on-encryption-to-recruit-americans-and-order-killings-20150708.

114 Rukmini Callimachi, "ISIS and the Lonely Young American," The New York Times, June 27, 2015, http://www.nytimes.com/2015/06/28/world/americas/isis-online-recruiting-american.html?_r=0.

115 Ibid.

116 Ibid.

117 Ibid.

118 Ibid.

119 Ibid.

120 Michael McCaul, "Europe Has a Jihadi Superhighway Problem," Time Inc., November 11, 2014, http://time.com/3578462/european-union-security-gap-foreign-fighters-terrorists/.

121 Findings and Recommendations regarding overseas security gaps which have facilitated this type of terrorist travel are outlined in the "Detection & Disruption" section of this report.

122 Task Force briefing, July 2015.

123 Cheryl K. Chumley, "U.S. Veteran: Going to Syria to Fight 'like Booking Flight to Miami Beach'," Washington Times, January 2, 2015, http://www.washingtontimes.com/news/2015/jan/2/us-veteran-going-to-syria-to-fight-like-booking-fl/.

124 Constanze Letsch, "UK Police Move to Take down Islamic State How-to Guide from Internet," The Guardian, February 25, 2015, http://www.theguardian.com/world/2015/feb/25/uk-police-islamic-state-travel-guide-hijrah-turkey-syria-ctiru.

125 "How to Survive in the West: A Mujahid Guide," 2015.

126 Countering Violent Islamist Extremism: The Urgent Threat of Foreign Fighters and Homegrown Terror House Committee on Homeland Security: Hearing Before the Committee on Homeland Security, House of Representatives, 114th Cong., 1st sess., February 11, 2015, http://homeland.house.gov/hearing/hearing-countering-violent-islamist-extremism-urgent-threat-foreign-fighters-and-homegrown.

127 The challenge of "broken travel" is covered further in this report in Key Finding 25.

128 James Dowling, "Jihadists Urged to Take European Holiday before Joining Islamic State to Avoid Raising Suspicion," Herald Sun, June 14, 2015, http://www.heraldsun.com.au/news/victoria/jihadists-urged-to-take-european-holiday-before-joining-islamic-state-to-avoid-raising-suspicion/story-fnpp4dl6-1227397514580.

129 United States of America v. Abdirahman Sheik Mohamud.

130 Alessandria Masi and Hanna Sender, "How Foreign Fighters Joining ISIS Travel To The Islamic State Group's 'Caliphate'" International Business Times, March 03, 2015, http://www.ibtimes.com/how-foreign-fighters-joining-isis-travel-islamic-state-groups-caliphate-1833812.

131 Ibid.

132 National Commission on Terrorist Attacks upon the United States, "What to do? A Global Strategy: Reflecting on a Generational Challenge," chap. 12, http://govinfo.library.unt.edu/911/report/911Report_

Ch12.htm.

133 National Security Intelligence Reform Act, 2004, Pub. L. No. 108-458, 108th Cong., http://www.dni.gov/files/documents/IRTPA%20 2004.pdf .

134 National Counterterrorism Center, "National Strategy to Combat Terrorist Travel." May 2, 2006. http://fas.org/irp/threat/travel.pdf.

135 The White House, "National Strategy for Counterterrorism," June 2011, https://www.whitehouse.gov/sites/default/files/counterterror-ism_strategy.pdf.

136 Individual departments and agencies have been tasked to determine how they can improve security to defend against the foreign fighter threat, and those reviews have produced notable enhancements in security. This is not the same, however, as producing a government-wide strategy that outlines all relevant programs, identifies gaps, and prioritizes resources.

137 See the "Americans on the Pathway to Terror: By-the-Numbers" sub-section of this report.

138 See "Appendix II: American Foreign Fighter Aspirants and Recruits" for the public cases the Task Force reviewed.

139 Michael S. Schmidt and Mark Mazzetti, "Suicide Bomber From U.S. Came Home Before Attack," The New York Times, July 30, 2014, http://www.nytimes.com/2014/07/31/us/suicide-bomber-from-us-came-home-before-attack.html?_r=0.

140 U.S. Department of Homeland Security, Federal Emergency Management Agency, "National Level Exercise 1009 Fact Sheet," 2009, http://www.fema.gov/txt/media/factsheets/2009/ncp_nle.txt.

141 The Task Force is grateful for the work of the Homeland Security Advisory Council, which recently put forward a similar recommendation. See: U.S. Department of Homeland Security, Homeland Security Advisory Council, "Foreign Fighter Task Force Interim Report," Spring 2015, http://www.dhs.gov/sites/default/files/publications/DHS-HSAC-Foreign-Fighter-Task-Force-Interim-Report-May-2015.pdf.

142 House Homeland Security Committee, Terror Threat Snapshot: September 2015.

143 SWJ Editors, "ISIS Publishes Manual on 'How to Survive in the West'," Small Wars Journal. June 9, 2015, http://smallwarsjournal.com/blog/isis-publishes-manual-on-%E2%80%98how-to-survive-in-the-west%E2%80%99.

144 Moore, "5,000 Foreign Fighters Flock to Libya as ISIS Call for Jihadists"; Julia Payne, "Exclusive: Captured Video Appears to Show Foreign Fighters in Nigeria's Boko Haram," Reuters, May 26, 2015, http://www.reuters.com/article/2015/05/26/us-nigeria-violence-for-eign-idUSKBN0OB1RR20150526.

145 Task Force briefing, July 2015.

146 9/11 Commission report, chap. 12, http://govinfo.library.unt.edu/911/report/911Report_Ch12.htm.

147 Ibid.

148 "Terrorist Watchlist," U.S. Government Sharing Environment. http://www.ise.gov/terrorist-watchlist.

149 White House. Summary of the White House Review of the December 25, 2009 Attempted Terrorist Attack, https://www.whitehouse.gov/sites/default/files/summary_of_wh_review_12-25-09.pdf.

150 U.S. Congress. Committee on Homeland Security. The Road to Boston: Counterterrorism Challenges and Lessons from the Boston Marathon Bombings, March 2014, 29-35. https://homeland.house.gov/sites/homeland.house.gov/files/docu-ments/Boston-Bombings-Report.pdf.

151 U.S. Government Accountability Office. Report to Congressional Requesters, Terror Watchlist: Routinely Assessing Impacts of Agency Actions since the December 25, 2009, Attempted Attack Could Help Inform Future Efforts, GAO-12-476 (Washington, DC, 2012), http://www.gao.gov/assets/600/591312.pdf.

152 "France Attack Suspect Unknown to U.S. Authorities," CNN, August 25, 2015, http://www.cnn.com/videos/tv/2015/08/25/new-day-savidge-france-supect-american-heroes-latest.cnn?sr=biob-armfeed.

153 GAO also flagged this problem in 2011, but the Task Force believes it persists. See: U.S. Government Accountability Office. Report to the Committee on Homeland Security and Governmental Affairs, U.S. Senate. Visa Waiver Program: DHS Has Implemented the Elec-tronic System for Travel Authorization, but Further Steps Needed to Address Potential Program Risks, GAO-11-335 (Washington, DC, May 2011), http://www.gao.gov/new.items/d11335.pdf.

154 Ibid.

155 Ibid. This concern was first flagged by GAO, but it appears to have persisted.

156 Currently around 50 member states have joined the initiative.

157 Information provided to Task Force staff by INTERPOL Washington in September 2015.

158 Task Force briefing with INTERPOL officials in France, May 2015.

159 See related finding from the Homeland Security Advisory Council: "Foreign Fighter Task Force Interim Report," Spring 2015.

160 U.S. Department of Homeland Security. Privacy Impact for the DHS Data Framework – Interim Process to Address an Emergent Threat, DHS/ALL/PIA-051, April 15, 2015, http://www.dhs.gov/sites/de-fault/files/publications/privacy-pia-dhswide-dataframework-april2015.pdf

161 This example is a hypothetical and was not provided by DHS.

162 Homeland Security Advisory Council, "Foreign Fighter Task Force Interim Report," Spring 2015.

163 Ibid.

164 This example was shared with the Task Force in April 2015 by Homeland Security officials.

165 Julia Payne, "FBI Investigating ISIS Suspects in All 50 States," The Hill, May 26, 2015, http://thehill.com/blogs/blog-briefing-room/233832-fbi-investigating-isis-suspects-in-all-50-states.

166 Task Force briefing, July 2015.

167 This is a reference to the Drug Abuse Resistance Education program; comments made by General Frank Taylor during the following hearing: House Committee on Homeland Security, Countering Violent Islamist Extremism: The Urgent Threat of Foreign Fighters and Homegrown Terror, 114 Cong., 1st sess., Doc. (Washington: Government Printing Office, 2015), http://www.gpo.gov/fdsys/pkg/CHRG-114hhrg94106/html/CHRG-114hhrg94106.htm.

168 Katie Zavadski, "Group With No Jihadi Experience Rehabs ISIS Recruit," The Daily Beast, August 24, 2015, http://www.thedailybeast.com/articles/2015/08/24/judge-orders-isis-recruit-to-rehab-not-jail.html.

169 Ibid.

170 Devlin Barrett, "FBI to Seek Counseling, Not Handcuffs, for Some Islamic State Suspects," Wall Street Journal, August 5, 2015, http://www.wsj.com/articles/fbi-to-use-counseling-not-handcuffs-for-some-islamic-state-suspects-1438812264.

171 Ibid.

172 Lorenzo Vidino and Seamus Hughes, Countering Violent Extremism in America, report, June 2015, https://cchs.gwu.edu/sites/cchs.gwu.edu/files/downloads/CVE%20in%20America%20.pdf

173 Joint Statement with Deputy Attorney General Sally Quillian Yates Before the Senate Judiciary Committee Washington, D.C., 114th Cong. (2015) (testimony of James B. Comey, Director, FBI).

174 See the "Americans on the Pathway to Terror: By-the-Numbers" sub-section of this report.

175 Task Force briefing, June 2015.

176 Greg Miller and Scott Higham, "In a Propaganda War against ISIS, the U.S. Tried to Play by the Enemy's Rules," Washington Post, May 8, 2015, https://www.washingtonpost.com/world/national-security/in-a-propaganda-war-us-tried-to-play-by-the-enemys-rules/2015/05/08/6eb6b732-e52f-11e4-81ea-0649268f729e_story.html.

177 Task Force briefing with CSCC officials, May 2015.

178 DHS, the State Department, and other government agencies routinely interact with Facebook, Twitter, Google, and other major social media players. However, other websites that are regularly used by extremists to share content, such as Ask.fm, reportedly have not been contacted by U.S. departments and agencies to participate in dialogue about removing terrorist propaganda.

179 Task Force briefing, May 2015.

180 For an example, see: U.S. Department of State, "Daesh Defectors: "I Was Afraid All the Time"" YouTube, July 24, 2015, https://www.

youtube.com/watch?v=j7AJfmpFakI.

181 Quilliam Foundation, "Quilliam Launches #NotAnotherBrother," news release, August 4, 2015, http://www.quilliamfoundation.org/press/quilliam-launches-notanotherbrother/.

182 Graeme Wood, "What ISIS Really Wants," The Atlantic, February 15, 2015, http://www.theatlantic com/magazine/archive/2015/03/what-isis-really-wants/384980/.

183 Revocation or Limitation of Passports, 22 CFR § 51.62 (2014).

184 Task Force Briefing with State Department, June 2015. Also see: Kent v. Dulles (June 16, 1958).

185 United States, Department of State, Passport Revocation - Anwar Nasser Aulaqi, , http://images.politico.com/global/2012/11/28/binder1.html.

186 U.S. Customs and Border Protection. "Border in Miles: How Long is the U.S. Border with Canada and Mexico?" July 30, 2013, https://help.cbp.gov/app/answers/detail/a_id/578/~/border-in-miles.

187 9/11 Commission report, chap. 12, http://govinfo.library.unt.edu/911/report/911Report_Ch12.htm

188 United States, Department of State, Immigrant and Nonimmigrant Visas Issued at Foreign Service Posts: Fiscal Years 2010 - 2014, http://travel.state gov/content/dam/visas/Statistics/AnnualReports/FY2014AnnualReport/FY14AnnualReport-TableI.pdf.

189 Task Force briefing with DHS and State Department, June 2015.

190 Ibid.

191 Written testimony of CBP Office of Field Operations Acting Deputy Assistant Commissioner for a House Committee on Oversight and Government Reform, Subcommittee on National Security hearing titled "Border Security Oversight, Part III: Border Crossing Cards and B1/B2 Visas," 113th Cong. (2013) (testimony of John Wagner).

192 Ibid.

193 Ibid.

194 Task Force briefing with DHS and the State Department, June 2015.

195 Ibid.

196 Over time, DHS should also examine how to deploy the system to all countries.

197 U S. Department of Homeland Security, Office of the Secretary, "Statement by Secretary Johnson on Security Enhancements to the Visa Waiver Program," news release, November 3, 2014, http://www.dhs.gov/news/2014/11/03/statement-secretary-johnson-security-enhancements-visa-waiver-program.

198 House Committee on Oversight and Government Reform, 113th Cong. (2013) (testimony of John Wagner).

199 U S. Department of State, "Visa Waiver Program," http://travel.state.gov/content/visas/english/visit/visa-waiver-program.html.

200 U.S. Department of Homeland Security, Office of the Secretary, "Statement by Secretary Jeh C. Johnson on Intention to Implement Security Enhancements to the Visa Waiver Program," news release, August 6, 2015, http://www.dhs.gov/news/2015/08/06/statement-secretary-jeh-c-johnson-intention-implement-security-enhancements-visa.

201 See the "Border Security" section of Key Finding 29 in this report.

202 James Meek, Cindy Galli, and Brian Ross, "Exclusive: U.S. May Have Let 'Dozens' of Terrorists Into Country As Refugees," ABC News, November 20, 2013, http://abcnews.go.com/Blotter/al-qaeda-kentucky-us-dozens-terrorists-country-refugees/story?id=20931131.

203 FBI Assistant Director for Counterterrorism Michael Steinbach made this point in a February hearing before the Committee: House Committee on Homeland Security, Countering Violent Islamist Extremism: The Urgent Threat of Foreign Fighters and Homegrown Terror, 114 Cong., 1st sess., Doc. (Washington: Government Printing Office, 2015), http://www.gpo.gov/fdsys/pkg/CHRG-114hhrg94106/html/CHRG-114hhrg94106.htm.

204 Subcommittee on Counterterrorism and Intelligence, House Committee on Homeland Security, Intelligence Sharing and Terrorist Travel, 112th Cong., 1st sess., H. Rept. (Washington: Government Printing Office, 2011), http://www.gpo.gov/fdsys/pkg/CHRG-112hhrg73736/html/CHRG-112hhrg73736.htm.

205 Carole Landry, "Foreign Fighters Switching Tactics to Reach Syria, Iraq," Yahoo News, May 29, 2015, http://news.yahoo.com/us-says-efforts-stop-foreign-fighters-fall-way-163730357.html.

206 House Committee on Homeland Security, Countering Violent Islamist Extremism: The Urgent Threat of Foreign Fighters and Homegrown Terror.

207 Ibid.

208 "DHS Announces Intent to Expand Preclearance to 10 New Airports," The Department of Homeland Security, May 29, 2015, http://www.dhs.gov/news/2015/05/29/dhs-announces-intent-expand-preclearance-10-new-airports.

209 UN Department of Public Information, "Security Council Unanimously Adopts Resolution Condemning Violent Extremism."

210 Ibid.

211 Lauren Frayer, "In Spanish Barrio, Residents Recall Train Attack Suspect Charged in France," Los Angeles Times, August 28, 2015, http://www.latimes.com/world/europe/la-fg-spain-france-train-attack- suspect-20150827-story.html.

212 Hijrah to the Islamic State, 2015.

213 Kim Willsher, "Islamic State Magazine Interviews Hayat Boumeddiene," The Guardian, February 12, 2015, http://www.theguardian.com/world/2015/feb/12/islamic-state-magazine-interviews-hayat-boumeddiene.

214 Due to the sensitivities of outlining intelligence and information-sharing gaps, the Task Force declines to identify specific partner countries by name, except where noted by public sources.

215 Maya Vidon-White and John Dyer, Special for USA TODAY, "Europe Shifts Policy in Escalating War on Terror," USA Today, January 25, 2015, http://www.usatoday.com/story/news/world/2015/01/25/european-civil-liberties/22117007/.

216 Task Force staff meeting with Turkish officials, July 2015.

217 Dave Keating, "EU Leaders to Call for Revision of Schengen Border Code," Politico, February 12, 2015, http://www.politico.eu/article/eu-leaders-to-call-for-revision-of-schengen-border-code/. Fortunately, this is not true for non-EU persons, who are typically screened against terrorist and criminal databases when they enter and exit the European Union.

218 Ibid.

219 European leaders are aware of this security gap and have put forward measures to do more checks "on the basis of a risk assessment," e.g. on individuals traveling from higher-risk locations. The Task Force believes such half-measures are woefully inadequate and that all EU nationals should be screened against terrorism watchlists when traveling to and from the continent.

220 Adrian Croft and Barbara Lewis, "EU Leaders Urge Stricter Border Checks in Counter-terror Drive," Reuters UK, February 12, 2015, http://uk.reuters.com/article/2015/02/12/uk-eu-security-leaders-idUKKBN0LG01H20150212.

221 As a result, the bulk of European passports do not get checked against INTERPOL's global Stolen and Lost Travel Document Database, a process which happens for anyone entering or exiting the United States.

222 EU officials are reportedly beginning to require more thorough inspections of EU passports in light of security concerns, but knowledgeable observers have reported to the Task Force that such changes do not appear to have widely taken effect.

223 Foreign Terrorist Fighters - Application of the Schengen Border Code - Follow-up - Update on Progress on the Preparation of Risk Indicators, report (Brussels: Council of the European Union, 2015), http://www.statewatch.org/news/2015/may/eu-council-ff-sbc-risk-indicators-8741-15.pdf.

224 Advance Passenger Information (API) data typically includes a passenger's flight information as well as information received by a passenger at the time of check-in on government-issued travel documents, including name and date of birth. Passenger Name Record (PNR) data is more detailed and is received by authorities earlier; it includes the information customers provide to airlines when they buy their tickets, including booking and payment details. This information is then used by law enforcement to screen passengers and assign risk profiles.

225 As of this writing, EU leaders are still in negotiations over an EU-wide PNR system. The issue has been debated within the European Parliament since 2011 but has been held up by member states over data privacy concerns.

226 "UN Urges Greater Use of Advance Passenger Information to Stem Flow of Foreign Terrorist Fighters," UN News Center, June 11, 2015, http://www.un.org/apps/news/story.asp?NewsID=51128#.Vd-PQTbJVikp.

227 Ibid.

228 "Country Reports: Europe Overview," U.S. Department of State, http://www.state.gov/j/ct/rls/crt/2014/239406.htm.

229 John Thor Dahleburg, "European Nations Unify Laws to Prevent Foreign Fighters," Yahoo News, May 19, 2015, http://news.yahoo.com/european-nations-streamline-laws-prevent-foreign-fighters-135730408.html.

230 However, the Swedish government has pledged to tighten its laws in the coming months to close gaps. See: Simon Johnson and Dominic Evans, "Sweden to Tighten Anti-terrorism Laws," Reuters UK, August 28, 2015, http://uk.reuters.com/article/2015/08/28/uk-sweden-security-idUKKCN0QX0QP20150828.

231 Ibid.

232 Task Force briefing with State Department, July 2015.

233 Alexandra Farone, "Bulgaria Justice Ministry Proposes Criminal Code Changes to Fight Terrorism," JURIST, March 10, 2015, http://jurist.org/paperchase/2015/03/bulgaria-justice-ministry-proposes-criminal-code-changes-to-fight-terrorism.php.

234 DOJ, Attorney General Holder Urges International Effort to Confront Threat of Syrian Foreign Fighters.

235 "Country Reports: Europe Overview," U.S. Department of State.

236 Mark Rivett-Carnac, "U.N.: 850,000 Refugees Are Expected to Reach Europe during 2015 and 2016," Time, September 9, 2015, http://time.com/4026046/refugees-migrants-europe-united-nations-crisis-greece-germany/.

237 Jack Crone, "ISIS Plotting Trojan Horse Campaign by Smuggling Militants into Western Europe Disguised as Refugees ," Mail Online, October 06, 2014, http://www.dailymail.co.uk/news/article-2782625/ISIS-plotting-Trojan-Horse-campaign-smuggling-militants-western-Europe-disguised-refugees.html.

238 "Islamic State Militants 'smuggled to Europe' - BBC News," BBC News, May 17, 2015, http://www.bbc.com/news/world-africa-32770390.

239 John Thor Dahleburg, "EU Official: Migrant Boats Also Carrying IS Fighters," The Big Story, July 6, 2015, http://bigstory.ap.org/article/29599fc513b8443085e63c60fbf11c3c/eu-official-terrorists-could-cross-mediterranean-europe.

240 The Associated Press, "Tunisia Museum Terror Attack Suspect Arrested in Italy," NY Daily News, May 20, 2015, http://www.nydailynews.com/news/world/tunisia-museum-terror-attack-suspect-arrested-italy-article-1.2229062.

241 Harald Doornbos and Jenan Moussa, "Italy Opens the Door to Disaster," Foreign Policy, April 13, 2015, http://foreignpolicy.com/2015/04/13/italy-islamic-state-syria-refugees/.

242 Ibid.

243 The 9/11 Commission Report, http://www.9-11commission.gov/report/911Report.pdf.

244 For instance, see: Tom Rayner, "Foreign IS Recruits Using Fake Syrian Passports," Sky News, February 25, 2015, http://news.sky.com/story/1433658/foreign-is-recruits-using-fake-syrian-passports.

245 Dipesh Gadher and Richard Kerbaj, "Islamic Militants Faking Deaths to Get Home, Say Security Sources," The Australian, June 22, 2014, http://www.theaustralian.com.au/news/world/islamic-militants-faking-deaths-to-get-home-say-security-sources/story-fn-b64oi6-1226962867588.

246 UN Department of Public Information, "Security Council Unanimously Adopts Resolution Condemning Violent Extremism."

247 Passport Control Mechanisms: The Most Significant Challenges, publication, 1st ed., vol. 10 (International Civil Aviation Organization), http://www.icao.int/publications/journalsreports/2014/MRTD_Report_Vol10_No1.pdf.

248 Tom Shiel, "Islamic State: Where Do Its Fighters Come From?," The Telegraph, June 8, 2015, http://www.telegraph.co.uk/news/worldnews/islamic-state/11660487/Islamic-State-one-year-on-Where-do-its-fighters-come-from.html.

249 Ibid.

250 Ibid.

251 Ibid.

252 Mike Giglio and Munzer Al-Awad, "How An American Tourist Lost His Passport In Istanbul And Was Sucked Into Syria's War," BuzzFeed, May 28, 2015, http://www.buzzfeed.com/mikegiglio/stolen-passports-and-isis-fighters#.qox7z1Myy.

253 Ibid.

254 Task Force staff site visit to INTERPOL Washington, June 30, 2015.

255 In 2012, INTERPOL's chief blasted countries for failing to use the system. See: Associated Press, "Interpol Chief: Countries Not Using Databases," Fox News, January 19, 2012, http://www.foxnews.com/world/2012/01/19/interpol-chief-countries-not-using-databases/.

256 Task Force briefing with INTERPOL Washington, June 4, 2015.

257 Ibid.

258 Elisha Fieldstadt and Becky Bratu, "Missing Passport Databases Not Routinely Checked: Interpol - NBC News," NBC News, March 14, 2014, http://www.nbcnews.com/storyline/missing-jet/missing-passport-databases-not-routinely-checked-interpol-n48261.

259 Task Force briefing with INTERPOL Washington, June 4, 2015.

260 The Task Force heard these concerns from multiple officials while examining security screening measures in Europe.

261 Associated Press, "Man Arrested in Tunisia Museum Attack Came to Italy on Migrant Boat," Fox News, May 20, 2015, http://www.foxnews.com/world/2015/05/20/italian-police-make-arrest-in-connection-with-tunisia-museum-attack/.

262 The Department recently announced plans to begin requiring VWP countries to screen against INTERPOL's Stolen and Lost Travel Document Database. See: "Statement by Secretary Jeh C. Johnson on Intention to Implement Security Enhancements to the Visa Waiver Program," news release, August 6, 2015, The Department of Homeland Security. http://www.dhs.gov/news/2015/08/06/statement-secretary-jeh-c-johnson-intention-implement-security-enhancements-visa.

263 "Programs and Initiatives," U.S. Department of State, http://www.state.gov/j/ct/programs/index.htm#TSI.; "Terrorist Interdiction Program (TIP)," U.S. Department of State, http://2001-2009.state.gov/s/ct/rls/fs/2002/12676.htm.

264 "Combating Terrorism: Additional Steps Needed to Enhance Foreign Partners' Capacity to Prevent Terrorist Travel," U.S. Government Accountability Office, June 30, 2011, http://www.gao.gov/products/ GAO-11-637.

265 Ibid.

266 This briefing was hosted by the Full Committee, rather than the Task Force.

267 Ibid.

268 This includes the age of the suspect at arrest, time of death, or other relevant incident. In some cases, the exact age is an estimate based on publicly available data.

www.ingramcontent.com/pod-product-compliance
Lightning Source LLC
Chambersburg PA
CBHW081416280526
45788CB00009B/3129